TEACHING OF ENGLISH

Published by
Lotus Press Publishers & Distributors

TEACHING OF ENGLISH

Rajinder Kumar

Lotus PRESS
4735/22, Prakash Deep Building,
Ansari Road, Daryaganj,
New Delhi - 110002

Lotus Press Publishers & Distributors
Unit No.220, 2nd Floor, 4735/22, Prakash Deep Building,
Ansari Road, Daryaganj, New Delhi - 110002
Ph.: 32903912, 23280047, 09811838000
E-mail : lotus_press@sify.com
Visit us : www.lotuspress.co.in

Teaching of English

ISBN: 81-8382-025-5

Published by : **Lotus Press Publishers & Distributors,** New Delhi-110002
Printed at : **A.J. Book Binding House**, Delhi

PREFACE

'Teaching of English' is a complete text-cum-reference book for teachers, teacher-trainers and teacher-trainees of all pedagogical institutes and departments of Education of different universities.

The present book is designed to highlight the important aspects of english language, traditional and structural approach, modern aids to teaching english, educational issues and teaching of english. This book can prove an effective guide to teachers and teacher-trainees for understanding the psychology of students and their problem and show the right path in the field of teaching.

This book deals with the topics of—English—The First Foreign Language; History of English Language; Educational Issues in Teaching of English; Methods of Teaching; Learning of English Language; Language Content and Kinds of Lessons; Concept of Language, Teaching and Learning; Process of Reading, Writing and Spellings; Audio-Visual Aids; Principles Governing the Choice of Textual Selections; Teaching of Grammar and Translation; Techniques of Teaching, Writing and Composition; Teaching of Literature and Prose; Teaching of Poetry and Other Activities; Teaching of Drama.

All the fundamentals of Teaching of English has been given in this book which have been drawn from authoritative sources. Yet the simple interpretation makes it an ideal text-cum-reference book.

Publisher

Contents

Preface *v*

1. English—The First Foreign Language 1
2. History of English Language 23
3. Educational Issues in Teaching of English 30
4. Methods of Teaching 47
5. Learning of English Language 65
6. Language Content and Kinds of Lessons 81
7. Concept of Language, Teaching and Learning 93
8. Process of Reading, Writing and Spellings 113
9. Audio-Visual Aids 140
10. Principles Governing the Choice of Textual Selections 159
11. Teaching of Grammar and Translation 175
12. Techniques of Teaching, Writing and Composition 194
13. Teaching of Literature and Prose 213
14. Teaching of Poetry and Other Activities 229
15. Teaching of Drama 241

1

English—The First Foreign Language

There is little doubt that the advent of the National Curriculum (NC) represents a major boost to the teaching of modern languages (MLs) in British secondary schools, though proposed slimming down of the curriculum may limit the achievement. The structure and design of the syllabus puts them in line with other areas of the curriculum, and they now enjoy the status of being a foundation subject. Although some will regret the failure to extend MLs to primary level (though there are a number of experimental courses attesting to interest in teaching foreign languages to younger learners), it does seem that MLs have come of age. It has not always been the case, however, that this area of the curriculum has promoted such a mood of optimism and expansion, and it is worth considering what has brought about this change.

Firstly, we should not underestimate the significance of the professional lobby. The status gained from having languages as an essential component of the NC is immense, and is a reflection of the hard work carried out by professional bodies over the years in making their case. This has not been easy in a country renowned for its reticence in learning languages other than English. It is not so long ago that learning foreign languages appeared elitist and their presence in the curriculum seemed under threat. It is a tribute to teachers enthusiasm for and commitment to teaching languages to all abilities and age groups that these fears have largely been allayed. An understanding of the importance of the future role of MLs is also evident in the NC's policy of languages for all, which ensures that, henceforth, all secondary school pupils will continue with at least one foreign language until the end of compulsory education. Teaching and motivating all pupils for a further two years, and aiming for realistic and useful levels of linguistic competence, presents a major challenge for all concerned in the teaching of languages. It is, then, this potential expansion in the scale of language teaching which partly explains the present energy and enthusiasm of the foreign language teaching world. The feeling seems to be that at last we have been given the opportunity to show what we can do.

These developments have come at an opportune time; and it is appropriate that the introductory year for the NC in modern languages should have occurred in 1992, the year of the free market, when issues concerning the future of the European community had a high profile in the popular media. Finally, it seems, the European idea has caught on in Britain. People are increasingly seeing Europe as a potential place of employment or residence. In these cases, languages increase possibilities and facilitate access. With this in mind, more students than ever before are opting to study languages at A-level and on undergraduate courses. Languages are seen as buying opportunities, as complementary skills worth the investment of time and effort. The atmosphere is therefore right for a new prominence to be given to teaching and learning foreign languages. Schools are turning toward their neighbours on the continent; for studies with European perspectives, for holidays, trips and exchanges, and for a wider view on the vocational landscape.

There are, then, a number of social, economic and educational factors involved in the apparent surge in interest for learning foreign languages. These also coincide with a particularly interesting time in the development of syllabus design and teaching methodology. It is only a few years ago that language examinations came on single sheets of paper, with a limited number of essay titles, and short prose translation passages. Listening comprehension was tested by teachers reading out dictations in often near phonetic expression of foreign vowels and consonants, and passages recounting bizarre happenings in an idealised world. Older learners remember the classic texts of Whitmarsh and the gothic script of German textbooks. Even the later modern so-called audio-visual approaches of the late 1970s and 80s were often based on cultural stereotypes of misleading simplicity, on animals who could talk, on language that was repetitious and alien to pupils' own world view. How often have we heard people claim not to be able to speak languages 'after having received an English education', or passing O-level but not being able to speak a word of the foreign tongue. The O-level oral exam could be the first time a pupil had actually been required to carry on a conversation with another, other than brief question/answer sessions in class or in short spells with the assistant. CSE was supposed to be an alternative but the emphasis was still on depersonalised language and rote memorisation. In the oral exam, candidates were required to remember over 100 questions and answers that covered such things as the height of the Eiffel tower or intricate exchange rate calculations.

GCSE (German Organisation) did much to change the situation. Firstly, all teaching and testing give equal weighting to reading, writing, speaking and listening. Moreover, there is a single grade structure—from A to G—which covers two levels: Basic or General and Extended or Higher. Perhaps the most significant change, however, is in the content of the syllabus. GCSE allots the highest possible prominence to the cultural appropriateness and authenticity of its teaching and testing materials. Pupil-as-tourist or host are key concepts, as is comprehensibility to a 'sympathetic native speaker'. GCSE has shaped the teaching and learning of foreign languages across the entire age range, and has encouraged the appearance of a plethora of course books and supplementary teaching materials containing every kind of cultural artefact and language representation from daily life. So tapes now come with built-in background noise, letters are printed in hard to read handwriting, and pupils are required to research and negotiate themselves through posters, brochures, weather forecasts and the like. In oral exams, they are given roles to play and asked to 'get by', to make themselves understood and to elicit specific pieces of information from their partners. When they write, it is often enough to simply get the message across; with grammatical accuracy and linguistic sophistication being increasingly required only as we ascend grade levels.

Such developments in syllabus design and application have run in parallel with changes in teaching methodology; the latter evolving, partly in response to such changes and partly as a result of our increasing understanding of how languages are best taught and learnt. Applied linguistic research expanded at an enormous pace in the 1970s and 80s. In the USA, researchers in an empirical, psychometric tradition amassed an enormous quantity of data, which they used to suggest that languages are best taught through exposure to and oral work within the foreign language. A famous writer (Krashen, 1981, 1982) popularised a controversial distinction between acquisition and learning, seeming to claim that objective, conscious learning of language rules and structure had little effect on the actual acquisition of true linguistic competence. He also went further, suggesting that such classroom preoccupations can have a very negative effect on the 'natural' processes of language learning, as they encourage overuse of what he called the 'monitor'; which we might understand as the conscious control of speech accuracy through attempted applications of and corrections to explicit knowledge about language. All of this work emphasised the fundamental, organic process of language learning: we need only to tap into this to become competent learners. In the UK a number of writers went in a similar direction. For the most part these came from a less empirically based tradition. Developments in the teaching of English itself began to stress the importance of pupils' own language, of exploratory talk in the acquisition of knowledge and the reduced importance of formal grammar teaching. In foreign language teaching, too, communication became the buzz-word. We can now see, with a historical perspective, how the popular, audio-visual techniques of the 60s and 70s did not prove to be the answer to language learning and teaching difficulties. These gave way to more direct methods which placed a large emphasis on the contextualised, oral presentation and practice of language structures. At the same time, a number of English writers were developing ideas which we would later designate as the Communicative Method or Approach. It is a moot point as to what extent such writers had direct influence on the teaching of foreign languages in the UK. They were often writing for an EFL world. Similarly, it must be said that much of the work in the USA was with adults learning English in universities, or second language contexts.

If ideas which encouraged the active, communicative use of language in foreign language learning were 'in the air', another major influence on our thinking came from the schools themselves; namely the Graded Objectives in Modern Languages (GOML) movement. In this case, the impetus for the idea came from teachers working in the classroom. Taking the principle, perhaps, from another skill based subject, music, the GOML movement presented the idea of learning languages in a series of graded steps. Tests were criterion-referenced, which is to say pupils passed when they had achieved success in the criteria set for a particular level. Significantly, it was the view that languages could be taught and learnt as a series of small packages. These packages were almost always based on practical, get-by-in language and personal details.

The NC represents the point we have reached in the evoluton. We might ask to what extent, and how, a nationally-prescribed syllabus can determine classroom methodology. In one sense the two must interact. It is true that the arrival of the NC stimulated discussion of the aims and objectives of language teaching; what should be taught and how. The NC certainly responds directly to a number of apparent criticisms levelled against GCSE; most noticeably the extra emphasis the NC places on the use of the target language in the classroom (and, presumably, in all test materials) and the broader range of topic areas now offered. The report on which the NC was formulated (DES/WO, 1990c) makes it clear that communication is considered to be a guiding principle in future work. 'Learning to use a foreign language,' it states, 'is learning to communicate in this language'. Communication is seen as not only an end but a means of achieving this end. 'Communication' and 'communicative approach' are ambiguous terms, and it is sometimes unclear exactly what is intended by them methodologically. The examples of good practice offered by the report are useful illustrations, but it is necessary for teachers to generate their own good practice, not merely mimic the successful lessons of others.

A recent concise account of the communicative approach lists ten key principles:

1. Intention to mean	6. Target language use
2. Information gap	7. Approach to error
3. Personalisation	8. Authenticity
4. Unpredictability	9. Speech *v.* writing
5. Legitimacy	10. Practice *v.* real language

This is a useful checklist, but it is sometimes difficult to see what the various features add up to in terms of actual lesson planning. Many teachers obviously interpret communicative language as employing as much target language and doing as much oral work as is possible. This also seems to be the mood of the NC. Important questions remain, however, concerning the relevance and appropriateness of such an emphasis, the place of other language skills, and the role of grammar and knowledge about language. Established course books such as *Tricolore* and *Deutsch Heute* are based around a grammar syllabus onto which personalised, cultural orientations have been grafted. More recent publications take a more flexible, often piecemeal, approach to grammar and language structure work, which emphasises the memorisation of pragmatically based language chunks and phrases. The problem of integrating active, oral and communicative work with structural language knowledge is therefore by no means solved. It could well be that the answer does not lie so much in the design of course materials, but rather the organization of the teaching and learning situation.

The Learner

In this section we want firstly to consider the context of language learning for pupils. We shall then focus on the feature of individual differences between learners; in particular, exploring learner strategies.

Learning Context

It must be recognized that of all subjects within the school curriculum, foreign languages have not enjoyed great popularity. The archetypical French classroom is one of endless chanting of verbs, incomprehensible grammar explanations and unachievable pronunciations. Mercifully such lessons are largely a thing of the past. Colourful new materials and bright, well equipped teaching rooms can make the whole experience of learning languages fun and appealing. It would be misleading, however, to claim that this was always the case, or even the norm in all our schools. We must accept that for many pupils languages remain the least favoured of their school studies. Pupils beginning secondary school in Year 7, and studying foreign languages for the first time, almost universally approach them with excitement and enthusiasm. For them it is a new opportunity to discover a fresh outlook on the world and try something from scratch.

The way the school cumculum is organized often mitigates against success in languages for many pupils. The comparison of language teaching in secondary schools to 'gardening in a gale' is now famous; with its picture of the fresh green linguistic shoots so painstakingly cultivated during lessons by the teacher being blasted away by the cold harsh gale of English that greets pupils as soon as they set foot into the corridor. Of course, we cannot keep them in linguistic incubators. This does raise questions concerning the appropriateness of the aims and objectives of secondary school language work. It may be true that the emphasis on grammar explanations and exercises of the past did instill a view of language lessons as abstract and difficult. However, even if we accept the need for maximum exposure to the foreign language as an alternative, the gardening-in-a-gale metaphor highlights the difficulty in arranging sufficient time in most secondary school contexts for this 'natural' process to occur.

Theoretical Input

One author in the field of individual differences in language learning begins his book on the topic by observing how much of the thrust of applied linguistic research has tried to discover similarities between learners; in other words, to establish a kind of learning universal. This is understandable enough; if we can ascertain exactly how languages are learnt, then it should be a short step towards designing an appropriate method to actualise the process. Yet, after many years of intensive research, it would appear that such a view is simplistic; learners do not all learn in the same way, there is no one method to language teaching. Skehan's book sets out to group together the various strands of a research tradition into individual differences. The research quoted often involves long and detailed accounts of statistical data analysis. This section is indebted to his work in collecting together others' findings. Here, we shall use some of these findings to link in with actual language teaching methodology and learning, and, in particular, to highlight various aspects of present approaches to language teaching. We shall firstly discuss such features as motivation, aptitude and cognitive learning styles before looking at individual learning strategies.

Motivation

Motivation and success are intimately connected, and whilst motivation is not enough to achieve success in language learning, the opposite would seem to be true; that without motivation, it is probably impossible to acquire competence. The Primary School language project of the 1960s seemed to flounder partly through lack of motivation on the part of pupils. But what is motivation?

The most important work in this area has been carried out by Robert Gardner. He defines it as follows:

Motivation = Effort + Desire to achieve a goal + Attitudes

We can see the inverse relationship between these conditions and likely success. But any optimum environment is difficult to pre-plan, based as it is in the general background of learners. Work on diversification has shown how important attitudes towards certain European nationals are in stimulating commitment to and application to language studies. People's and pupils' motivation for learning languages, then, varies considerably; in some cases, it is for purely instrumental reasons, like the enhancement of job prospects. Yet this is likely to be too long-term for most pupils, and there must be some more immediate pay-off for the effort demanded. The GOML movement addressed the question of motivation head on, by responding to the acute difficulty of maintaining interest and effort in a subject when the main assessment was at the end of five years—the O-level. It might be felt that this is true of any subject, but language competence seems always to be measured against perfect native competence. GOML succeeded in instilling a sense of achievement in the attainment of much more modest levels of proficiency, by rewarding success in small, incremental stages, and thus providing more immediate motivation.

Language learning has also traditionally been characterised by a pre-occupation with the correction of error. It is still the belief of many language teachers that their job is to correct mistakes and that without correction learners cannot be expected to learn. Or worse that learners will adopt incorrect forms into their speech. Yet nothing is likely to have a more negative effect on motivation than for faults to be constantly pointed out. Here, balance is all. A skilled teacher knows how and when correction is appropriate. GOML avoided this over-correction. It also set the pattern of short, achievable steps towards language competence. Certification also occurred at regular, annual intervals. This works where pupils are motivated by academic success, but otherwise there is nothing intrinsically motivating about qualifications. Finally, no matter how much effort goes into parcelling learning into manageable pieces, it is the actual content of learning materials which has a determinate effect on enhancing motivation and consequent success.

Course books and teaching materials have improved enormously over recent years; colour is now common, music is based on disco and pop style, illustration and graphic design is lavish. The content of books places a high premium on authentic information and stories to represent the language, and they frequently use adolescent interests and pre-occupations. There is a danger that as this becomes the norm, the positive effects of such factors simply wear off. Similarly, it is all very well for teachers and publishers to pick out interesting features of a country, but this interest often depends on an experience and sensitisation which language specialists share, but has yet to come within the world life of pupils. In this case, such representations are simply obscure and alienating. It has become a cliche that pupils spend much of their time ordering meals they will not eat, planning journeys they will not take and making judgements they have yet to formulate in their own language, let alone another foreign one. There is indeed still much that can be done to improve motivation—trips and exchanges are obvious ways to make the language come alive. It is also important to have lively and attractive teaching exercises and materials.

Language Aptitude

Is there such a thing as language aptitude? If there is, how is it made up? Carroll lists four components to it:

1. Phonemic coding ability; or the ability to link foreign sounds to symbols—to identify and recall them.

2. Inductive language learning ability; or the ability to spot patterns of correspondence and relationship in language material—both syntactically and semantically.

3. Grammatical sensitivity; or the ability to recognise the grammatical function of words in sentences.

4. Memory and learning; or the ability to commit language 'information' to memory.

We all know that everyone within normal limits of intelligence can learn a foreign language in the natural environment. But away from this, otherwise extremely intelligent and gifted individuals sometimes have enormous difficulties in acquiring linguistic competence in a formal setting. They just do not 'get it' or are 'no good at languages'. In these cases, their minds do not seem to work that way. This has been more formally explored in such research as that of Brown and Witkin. Based on psychological studies they propose two types of cognitive characteristics: field independence and field dependence, which refer to the ways individuals think about and mentally organise the world. In tests field independent (FI) individuals are more able to distinguish features in a field, whilst field dependent (FD) individuals to not, but see it holistically. The writers conceptualise that FI Individuals are more analytic, more detached and impersonal. FD individuals, on the other hand, are more person orientated, sensitive and emotionally attached. In language learning terms, FDs being more person orientated, will be communicative and conversational. Conversely, FIs will have greater analytic and organising abilities.

The research area is fraught with test design problems and the justification for claims made is debatable. Also, compensatory exercises and activities designed to enhance previously identified aptitude deficiencies of learners, have been disappointing in terms of subsequent improvements in language competence. Still, it is helpful to meditate on these features. It is certainly within the range of the experience of every language teacher that some learners have a better 'ear' for the spoken word than others. This is bound to be of significance if the method being adopted is one that places emphasis on exposure to the oral expression of the language, leaving grammar to be understood on the basis of induction. Similarly, experience would corroborate research conclusions that explicit grammar explanations. This does not 'make sense' for some learners, and therefore cannot be operationalised. Other research (Wesche,

1981) has drawn the obvious conclusion from this and shown with some success that matching teaching methodology to learning style can enhance acquisition rate. What is clear from this research on individual differences in language learning is that we are not dealing with a uniform process, and there are social, cultural and psychological factors that have a determinate effect on the outcome of any methodological approach.

Teaching Strategy

At the beginning we discussed the general background to recent developments in syllabus design enshrined in the NC, with the particular intention of highlighting the problems thrown up by these changes for actual language learning and teaching activity. We then considered the case of the learner; focusing on individual experiences and differences, and examining learner strategies. We shall now turn to the implications of such aspects of language learning for methodological and innovation within the evolution of classroom practice under the influence of the NC. To summarise the various arguments so far:

* The NC presents us with a challenge to formulate new approaches for teaching modern languages in British secondary schools.
* The model of language learning implicit in the NC is, however, not precise.
* Past years have seen enormous moves forward in curriculum design and assessment procedures. Many current teaching materials are lively and attractive.
* The type of methodology used to teach the NC is also still ill-defined, and is often based on euphemisms and bland declarations, but is loosely termed 'communicative'.
* Past developments in foreign language learning and teaching in schools have done much to address issues of motivation, relevance, authenticity, etc. The problem of

face validity for pupil remains, as does the question of coping with individual differences in language classrooms.

* Important questions about the role of grammar can be left unresolved in a simplified, idealised model of communicative language teaching, as can the way to develop generative language use and the significance of pupils' knowledge about language.

Faced with the above, it may be useful to list the kind of principles on which language learning and teaching might be based. We would suggest the following:

That language teaching is about speaking and using the language.

That language learning should be about the expression of individual identity.

That language learning is about 'making sense'—in both productive and receptive senses of the expression.

That we should aim as far as possible to teach learners to generate their own language.

That pattern seeds can be sown and pupils slowly sensitised to grammatical differences and applications.

That all lessons needs structuring, both organisationally and linguistically, if teaching is to be effective.

That formal grammar explanations may be eschewed but generative language means having structures and patterns that are transformable. It is not enough to have a large list of stock phrases.

That knowledge about language comes about from reflections on language in use.

Learner Strategies

Let us now look at an area which may be more accessible to influence within a pedagogic framework; namely, learner strategies.

Research into this area offers the opportunity of discovering how language learners actually learn. Many individual differences are of a deep psychological type; possibilities for effecting change on these are therefore slim. Research that has been carried out in this field has rather suggested that we go against natural learning tendencies at our peril, and learners themselves are often the best judges of how they learn effectively. Strategy use, however, does highlight particular learning habits of pupils and students. If we can identify these in good learners, perhaps we can objectify them and teach them to all. A strategy might commonly be defined as an intelligent plan or method, or as the art of employing plans towards achieving a goal. A communication strategy is understood as the various ploys, or means, by which individuals exercise some control over discourse. As one author (Bialystok) insists, they are always interactive. Filler phrases are a good example of a communication strategy. These are means that are used to make space and time within a conversation; for example, repetition and intonation to gain clarification and elucidation, giving definitions as a means to seeking specific vocabulary, etc. These occur in native speaker situations, of course, but we can see how crucial they might be in foreign language discourse as a means of maintaining coherence and cohesion in speech. They are an important source of learning, and it is clear that those adept at employing them will gain much from a communicative type approach to language learning. However, attempts to teach them to students as a means of enhancing learning have not yielded encouraging results. This may be because such strategies are very much dependent on a learner's personality and individual psychology. They arise in spontaneous speech which is almost impossible to bring under conscious control.

In contrast, learner strategies are defined as the habits and practices adopted by learners in learning a second language. They can include anything that learners do, so it is not surprising that writers in the field have had such problems categorising them and presenting them in a systematic manner. Early work (Stern) tried to identify the sorts of strategies good language learners use: planning strategy, Empathetic strategy, Communicative strategy, etc. Later, systematic interviews and questionnaires were used to find out exactly what successful learners do to acquire linguistic competence. Again, it was found that learners did a little of everything, as needs be. It must be emphasised that the context of all of this work is crucial. Much of it was carried out in ESL/EFL situations and/or with adults. Where children were studied, it was often in an ESL situations where group dynamics and sociability were all important. In such cases, communication strategies are important, and language is acquired slowly as a kind of socio-communicative habit.

Other work (Rubin) has a different focus, concentrating much more on formal learning situations. Learners are asked to note particular practices in the course of their language studies. Many tens of habits and practices are referred to in work, far too many to be ever able to teach to others. Eventually lists of 'good' habits are drawn up; for example:

* use clues to guess meaning;
* compare native with foreign language;
* ignore word order;
* infer grammatical rule by analogy; and
* look up word in dictionary.

Compared with communication strategies, this type of learner strategy deals with language in a much more analytical, systematic way. Many learner strategies might even be understood as broadly based on more general study skills. In the context of teaching secondary school pupils foreign languages, the following questions become apparent:

* Which of the many strategies identified are applicable to secondary school pupils?
* How can we categorise these strategies?

* To what extent is it possible to teach these strategies, and which are most appropriate for the various methodological approaches we might use?
* Is there a developmental sequence in strategy use and does this vary with age?

We might begin to list such strategies as ways of organising work, asking for clarification, finding out meaning, monitoring progress, etc. It is possible that these could be taught in an explicit way. They could be systematised and inculcated in learners' learning habits in the course of teaching. They are not so dependent on personality and the spontaneity of speech or real-life situations as communicative strategies. Learners can therefore learn and make themselves use them. In other words, by making the unconscious, automatic habits of the good language learners available to all, we might be making many more good learning practices available to all. Moreover, by using them, learners begin to use language more spontaneously. This enhances the use of communicative strategies, and hence increases the rate of language acquisition. Much work still needs to be done to identify the strategies appropriate for various learners in school, to ascertain which comes first and to what extent these can be systematically taught.

Communicative Approach

Many methods and approaches are evident in use in our schools today. The most recently popular communicative approach has concentrated on oral exposition in the target language. A stereotypic lesson is likely to be composed of oral presentations followed by oral practice by pupils. This would be followed by oral feedback or some kind of writing/reading consolidation exercise. Most of the work makes great use of authentic materials and focuses on the national culture of the country whose language is being studied. Yet experience shows such lessons can also often get reduced to the rote memorisation of stock phrases and the creation of a world of make-believe that becomes disconnected from pupils' own experiences. As such it is just as boring and demotivating as any grammar/translation lesson. The NC has partly recognised this by broadening out the areas of experience to include creativity, imagination, the environment, the world of work, communications and technology. Perhaps, then, we can forget the stereotypic role-plays to which we have all become so accustomed. Changes in the topics of the syllabus content are not enough. Real advances in language learning must be about the realisation of improved pedagogic action. In the past, we have perhaps been over-reliant on a single approach to language learning throughout all years in the secondary school. Differences from one year to the next have been expressed in terms of topic, grammatical and the functional-notional content of the syllabus.

Grenfell has tried to describe the way the orientation of language lessons may evolve in the course of pupils' learning. He describes these as cycles: introduction, orientation and specialisation. The term cycle was employed partly to argue that any one cycle should include components of the other two, that these will cross year boundaries and that the accent for classroom activity will alter as pupils progress. Thus, the very first lessons should aim at getting the message across to learners that language lessons are about speaking and using the language, and that language is another source of individual expression and imagination. This slowly gives way to exercises aimed at raising awareness of learning strategies and sensitisation to patterns in language. The latter are seen as sowing the seeds, which may be taken up as explicit grammar rules later in the course. Finally, there is an orientation cycle which directs pupils to the type of final language work and assessment which they will meet.

Scaffolding Structures

Changes in methodology for teaching the NC can therefore come from established practice. Recent workers on the psychological ideas of Vygotsky have been keen to map out the classroom as an experience of shared understanding between teacher and taught and between pupils; in other words of 'common knowledge' (Edwards and Mercer). Much is made by them of this shared discourse and of the 'handing over' of knowledge. The necessary 'scaffolding' must be developed as organisational and discoursal structures to support this handing over. These may be contained in the planned activity of a lesson, in the elements of a conversation designed to enhance communicative strategies, or a set of linguistic problems given to help develop the learner strategy of, for example, dictionary use. Such scaffolding structures are crucial in the language classroom. Even an old technique in direct language teaching such as three-stage questioning offers insight into the innate dynamic in these structures. In this case, after oral presentation of, for example, a vocabulary item such 'a dog' through flashcard generated repetition, the sequencing of questioning would proceed as follows:

1. This is a dog, yes or no?
2. This is a dog or a cat?
3. What is this?

This may appear simplistic and naive. It is surprising, however, with pace, how such a series of vocabulary items can be worked on with energy and dynamism. Of course, it is not particularly progressive nor individualised, and yet it has proven to be popular and successful with generations of teachers and pupils. It is easy to see why, for the teacher can grade the difficulty of the question by the intended response. In *1.* just recognition is required on hearing the word and seeing the symbol. In *2.* the pupil sees the symbol and hears the word, and has to select (and importantly) say the given word, expression or phrase. In *3.* recognition must be followed by remembering the target language expression and its correct pronunciation. If there is a problem, then the next level of difficulty is reverted to until a correct answer is given. This is a good example of how the inner character of a particular language sequence can offer varying degrees of support to the learner.

Autonomy

The NC is, therefore, overly vague about methodology. The communicative approach, as popularly understood, is unlikely to be enough to cope with the flexibility required in future language classrooms. A more cyclic approach, based on varying activities according to learners development may well offer an improved method. Similarly, much can be gained from a deeper knowledge of classroom structures. However, there is still a need to search for other ways of getting learners in touch with, the language and managing their own learning. Present dissatisfactions with existing materials and methods have led some teachers to adopt more autonomous approaches for learners. It is possible that many of the characteristics of good language teaching and learning are realisable through these approaches. How so? The term itself is ambiguous, and might refer to total pupil liberty to set syllabus content and teaching methods, or to more restrained moves to increase choice in limited aspects of the teaching programme. There are two distinct components here; namely autonomous learning and autonomous teaching. By autonomous learning we understand any situation in which pupils can make free choices about what they do and say. An open-ended role-play is, in one sense, autonomous if pupils have the freedom and space to create their own language content and expression. On a more organised level, language learning through various drama exercises and techniques enable pupils to develop their own linguistic independence. Autonomous teaching, on the other hand, is almost a contradiction in terms, but may refer to the organisation of time and space to facilitate pupils' autonomy. We can identify three common models:

(a) ***The Carousel:*** In this case there are a number of separate language activities available at any one time in the class-room; for example, there might be a computer game, a role-play, a listening exercise, some reading to do, etc. Activities which cover different language skills are made available to pupils, and they work through them more or less at their own speed. The autonomy lies in the pace of work and the fact that pupils have to negotiate and solve their own on-the-spot problems.

(b) ***The Project:*** Here a specific topic area is chosen and then a set of activities and exercises devised so that pupils ascertain certain pieces of information they need for the task in hand. This could be planning a trip to Europe, in order to be interviewed for a job, researching something like the listening and viewing habits of fellow pupils and making comparisons with a European exchange school. Pupils might work through details at their own pace, and individually make choices about the sort of pieces of information they require and what they are going to do with them.

(c) ***Guide to Materials:*** In this model teachers supply guides for linking various course book chapters along with other material sources. This enables the teacher to select points where pupils make choices about what to do next—pupils can then work at their own pace.

All three standard models provide opportunities for differentiation, and pupils can work at a level appropriate to them. Clearly, some model activities enable pupils to give their own opinions and wishes, whilst others restrict self-expression. There is then individualisation of pace, topic, expression, activity. This varies between models and from activity to activity. There are important decisions to be made concerning the time that teachers need for the preparation of each of these; a series of exercises based on original authentic source materials is clearly going to take up more preparation time than a guided work sheet. A carousel of activities may take substantial time for organisation depending on school and departmental logistics. There are clearly pros and cons for the different models. Examples of their application in British schools emphasise the importance of finding operational frameworks with which both staff and pupils can feel unthreatened and confident. All of the models presented are, of course, limited in their scope for autonomy. It becomes evident that we are not in an either/or situation, and it is perfectly possible to combine both standard teacher input sessions and more autonomous activities. One project conducted in a group of London schools gives an indication of what is involved in moving teachers and pupils into increased group work and limited autonomy. Conclusions would seem to indicate that such work does indeed have a positive effect on motivation and involvement. However, later reflections suggest that more attention needs to be given to the processes of language teaching involved in such approaches. In short, why should autonomy and group work facilitate language learning? Which strategies and practices do pupils need to possess in order to operate in such an environment? Changes in the structural arrangement of lessons are therefore not enough; pupils also need to be trained to operate effectively and efficiently on their own. Initially, some consideration has to be given to making the reasons for such arrangements perfectly clear to pupils. Ground rules for activity in the classroom must be set. Leni Dam calls them the ten commandments; for example:

* speak as much target language as possible;
* be prepared in every lesson;
* make sure you know what you are doing; and
* ask three other pupils and use a dictionary before asking the teacher.

Pupils also need to carefully record what they have achieved, what was difficult for them, what they need to work on, how, and the result of the assessment tasks they have carried out. Constant feedback is also necessary in order to ascertain where pupils are at and what they are going to do next. Specific quizzes and questionnaires can be supplied to pupils for them to focus their thought on just what their classroom practice is. It is also possible to start giving pupils the kind of language learning strategies referred to earlier; for example, to practise role-plays pupils might:

* make up a jumble or a jigsaw of the words and then put them back in order;
* practise with a friend; and then
* listen over and over again to a tape;
* act it out using props to make it seem real.

Or, to polish up writing, pupils might:

* take a text and substimate their own words; and then
* use a word processor to draft and redraft a story;
* do a gap-fill exercise.

All of these strategies begin to enable pupils to work on their language work without constantly being organised by the teacher. We might start categorising such activities in developmental sequences, making decisions about what should be taught first, which can be made explicit to whom, and how far we can instill such practices through deliberately designed teaching activities. These can start to move learners from learning to acquisition, from controlled to automatic language use, from conscious to unconscious knowledge about language.

❐

2

History of English Language

Language is a means of communication through a system of symbols, in which each language has its own life and vitality—its own unique personality and distinctive character that cannot be interchanged with any other language as the nature and character of the English language is closely intertwined with, the British life, history and culture as portrayed in English literature. In this way the language of an individual sets his style of life itself and influences the very personality and make-up of a person. A newborn's communication in life with his environment comes through his various senses. The most predominant place is occupied by language, and very soon, a child learns to understand and speak in spite of his as yet undeveloped intellect. The most powerful motivating force at this stage, is the gregarious impulse. Man is basically a social animal. The necessity is to communicate with members of the family and to participate in the ideas, feelings, actions and emotions of others. This social participation enriches his mind with experiences. The enriched mind picks up various words and sounds in the environment. This process of the early development of language is purely imitative and wholly conscious under normal circumstances. The act of imitating the elders, when frequently repeated, takes the form of a habit. But his imitative and habitual acts are not wholly reproductive. He constructs his own structures and sentences though grammatically wrong, and coins his own structures, sentences and phrases to explain new situations.

The history of the growth of language is the history of the growth of man's intelligence. Man's superiority over the rest of the animal kingdom is mainly due to language. Speech is essentially a human faculty. It is an extremely complicated mental phenomenon involving the functions of neuro-motor apparatus for uttering meaningful sounds *i.e.* vocal symbols, auditory recognition, interpretation of visual impressions etc.

Human language has kept pace with the growth of civilization, and the character of English today is immensely richer than what it was a century or two centuries ago. In the same way language keeps pace with the growth of individual man. In the beginning, the child deals only with concrete objects, and his vocabulary is limited to those things which can be seen, heard or felt later. He learns to deal with abstract ideas. Education enriches these ideas and his enriched vocabulary helps him to broaden the horizons of his intellect and knowledge. Several machines like language—the telephone, radio, TV, movies, tape recorders, gramphones etc. have given added dimensions too.

The German scholar Goethe rightly remarked: "He who knows no foreign language knows nothing of his own." Intellectual growth is shaped by the language habits formed by the child from his very childhood through interrelation with society and the community. The growth of the intellect also depends a great deal upon language abilities. Intellect assumes concrete form through language—a medium of contact with knowledge, tradition and developments. In this way language helps an individual to acquire various abilities and solve complex problems. It is thus not only a means of communication in the field of technology, science, and other branches of knowledge. A facile language rich in literature and tradition is of tremendous values to the intellectual and emotional development of a person.

Language in school has a twofold role to play. It serves as a vehicle of thought and communication for acquiring knowledge of various subjects. For this a rich and varied language is both necessary and useful. In addition language is studied for its own sake. Its literature and the ornamentation of the language are useful for their own sake and contribute greatly to the smooth development of the individual. The imbibing of a nation's culture, traditions and customs is achieved through the study of language, and thus not only is it a means to an end, but it is a worthy end in itself also.

In the classroom and in school, imagination and intellect of the students help each other by establishing the normal social interplay of language. Work done in pairs or groups is more profitable and useful than work done alone. Moreover, the standard of the school has a tremendous influence on the upliftment or dropping of a child's intellectual and moral development.

In society, language is an essential requirement. According to Ben Jonson, "Speech is the instrument of society." It is not only the means of communication but it joins man to man by way of greetings, conversation, enquiries, cooperation, discussion and opposition. Language has thus a broader scope—it is a means of social control. The written and the spoken words exercise a very strong influence on the emotional arousal of the spirit. Works of Lincoln and Macaulay gave rise to the Indian Renaissance. Ideas emerge and materialise through language.

Historical Background

English was introduced into India almost two centuries ago with the advent of the East India Company and the Britishers. Originally, it played an important role in the trade and commerce of the country, but gradually, with the British assuming the role of rulers, English acquired a very important place in the political and educational life in the country. The British rulers needed more and more white collared clerks to run the administration of the country, and hence knowledge of English soon became a passport to government jobs and elite society. As Macaulay is known to have pointed out, English education aimed at producing "a class of people, Indian in blood and colour, but English in taste, in opinions, in morals and in intellect". English thus became the *"lingua franca"* of the country, the most important medium for education, trade, commerce, law and administration in India. The aim of teaching English was to give Indians a glimpse into the vast storehouse of English knowledge and literature.

English in India After Independence

After Independence in 1947, there were quite a few Indians who advocated the quitting of English from India with the British. This cry for the abolition of English had its root in the bitterness that had accumulated after a long period of British domination and exploitation. There were however, a few far-sighted leaders like Pandit Jawaharlal Nehru, the first Prime Minister of independent India, and Maulana Abul Kalam Azad, the first education minister, who felt that if English was done away with, the work of more than a century would seriously effect the education in the country. It was observed that this was akin to "throwing out the baby with the bath-water".

In the words of Pandit Nehru, "We are naturally driven to it principally because we know it a good deal, we have people who can teach it, and because it is the most important language in the world today."

It was generally agreed that pushing out English from India would only result in a grave loss to ourselves. As the Indian University Commission appointed soon after Independence to look into this problem, pointed out:

> "If under sentimental urges we should give up English, we should cut ourselves off from the living stream of our growing knowledge......English is the only means of preventing our isolation from the world, and we will act unwisely if we allow ourselves to be enveloped in the folds of the dark curtain of ignorance."

But men while advocating the continuance of English in the political and educational set-up of the country, our educational planners realised that English could not continue to enjoy the same place as it did during the British regime, as the lingua franca of the country. That role would sooner or later have to be given to a native Indian language. There are several lessons for the continued study of English in India, and which determine the new status that must be assigned to English in the educational pattern in the country.

CONTINUANCE OF ENGLISH IN INDIA

English language plays a wide and varied role in literature. It is considered powerful and flexible vehicle of thoughts and communication, and today enjoys the role of being almost a world language. There are various reasons, in addition to these that merit the continued study of English an important place in our educational system.

1. **Role of Language to get Independence:** It is indeed a paradox that the language that was hated the most by Indians was itself instrumental in gaining Indians their independence. English helped fan the spirit of nationalism in our leaders which ultimately freed the country from the British yoke. It was through English that our freedom fighters drew their inspiration from the writings of great thinkers like Abraham Lincoln, Carlyle, John Stuart Mill, Burke and others.

2. **Medium of International Link:** English today is almost a world language. It is the first language of United Kingdom, USA, Australia and New Zealand. It is the second language as understood in most Asian countries, Canada, South Africa, and many European countries and British colonies. Although Chinese is a language spoken by the maximum number of people in the world, this is due to the nature of their vast population, and it is confined only to China. English is the language spoken and understood in the maximum number of countries spread over the whole globe, and by a vast majority of different nations and communities. Knowledge of English is therefore, essential for establishing cultural, intellectual, economic, commercial and political relations with a major part of the world. It also helps us keep in touch with the world's ever-increasing explosion of knowledge and technological advancement, which are so important to a developing young nation like India.

3. **A Unifying Force:** English also served as a great unifying force in our struggle for independence. It is through this language that leaders from different corners of our vast country could communicate and plan their freedom struggle. In the present day set-up too, after almost four decades of independence, English is the only link as the medium for inter-state correspondence, and as the language for trade, commerce, industry and administration between different states in the country. In fact it is due to English alone that we continue to enjoy a unique "unity in diversity".

English is a necessary medium of communication for all competitive examinations. It provides a common yardstick for evaluation of candidates for Central government services. If selections for these services were done on the basis of regional languages, there would be a great disparity in results, leading to irregularities and communalism which act as divisive forces. Although the desirability of creating a native language such as Hindi as a unifying force has been felt, the time is not yet ripe, due to the resentment of the states in the south.

4. **Role of English in University Education:** English is the only suitable medium of instruction for advanced studies at university level. It is the necessary and desirable medium for all higher legal, technical, scientific and medical education and research, as most advanced knowledge in these fields is available in English. No regional language, not even Hindi, has as yet been able to make available all this knowledge in that language. Moreover, a common medium of instruction is essential at university level to prevent the country from offering for a dangerous fragmentation of academic life. Exchange of scholars in all academic fields, both national and international, would only be possible if English continues to enjoy an important place in the higher academic life in the country.

5. **A Beautiful Foreign Language:** There can be no denying that the study of English is worthwhile to Indians for its own sake, apart from the important role it has played in the historical past. It is a language rich in literature and power expression. It provides the

student with a flexible vehicle of thought and communication, giving him the power to reason and judge with critical balance.

English has greatly influenced and enriched Indian languages and literature. Some of the best known and loved writers of English have been Indians *e.g.* Rabindranath Tagore, Sarojini Naidu, Dr Radhakrishnan and Jawaharlal Nehru, who have contributed some immortal writing to English literature.

6. **Position in the School Curriculum:** The Constitution of India, adopted in 1950, had envisaged Hindi as the only official language of the Union of India, while English was to continue for 15 years. This was vehemently opposed by the states in the south. As a result, English was adopted as the Associate Official Language by an Act of Parliament in 1963. The position given to English in the school curriculum was clearly laid down by the Kothari Commission (1964-66), on the recommendations of which the school syllabi in most Indian states have been framed. There is a change in the objectives of teaching English too under the present conditions.

It is now realised that the teaching of English should be made more practical and language-oriented in order to achieve the limited objectives of learning this important foreign language. As it was pointed out by the Official Language Commission, "English has to be taught hereafter principally as language of comprehension rather than as literary language" so as to develop in the students learning it, a faculty for comprehending writings in the English language, more especially those relating to the subject matter of their specialised fields of studies.

❐

3

Educational Issues in Teaching of English

The history of education shows clearly that the school does not promptly react to changes in social demands; educational readjustment is seldom gradual and desirable changes in education gradually increase in number and importance until by the pressure of accumulated force that compel extensive and radical reorganisation at irregular intervals. A gradual and continuous readjustment to the changing demands of a dynamic society should be the characteristic of education at all times. Perfect conditions have never been obtained and in all probability the future will fail to provide them. The two very important and comprehensive landmarks on educational policy-making in India, were the Secondary Education Commission Report (1952-1953) and the Kothari Education Commission Report (1964-1966). The trend of secondary education in free India received a direction from the Secondary Education Commission Report undoubtedly, whereas, the Kothari Commission Report envisaged a total and comprehensive outlook and change throughout the education ladder from the early years to the stage of university education. There was clear evidence that the present is one such period when the accumulation of long-needed changes is likely to compel radical readjustment in the secondary school as well as in various other dimensions of the system of education. Even education came to be recognised and accepted as an important instrument for 'national development'. In fact, numerous factors combine to bring about extensive changes in the character of secondary education. The secondary school as a social institution is undergoing a marked transformation that necessitates important changes in its aims and functions to bring out contributions to national development. The number of school attenders is ever swelling from thousands to lakhs, requiring accommodation and infrastructural changes for a larger number of pupils. Such a development is also significant of the fact that large numbers of pupils are entering the secondary schools whose different capacities, interests and probable future activities demand differentiated forms of education.

The very broad contexts that influence language learning are those of psychology of individual differences on the one hand, and methods of quantitative measurement on the other. A re-examination of the laws of learning is truly at the bottom the cause of concern for the organisation of materials and methods of teaching English. Over that past four/five decades the pendulum has tilted on either side from time to time, seldom producing the desirable results. Added to the factors of educational psychology are the influences of sociological paradigm. It is as complex as it is varied. Sociological perspectives bring forth numeracy as well as divergence in the nature of the learner-groups, their subject values, tneir aspirations and needs, followed by the examination and realisation of vocational training, educational guidance and personnel preparation etc. Sociology further points out its one finger to the spread of population in rural and urban areas, amongst the rich and the poor, literate and would-be-literate mass of people and the other finger to the complex relations and interactions that are ever widening. The need for greater, wider and much varied communication is felt. At every minute of every dealing there is the need to use a language. In short, the extension of educational opportunities through the vast area of this country would require constant and continuous revision of aims and functions as much as redirection of methods of teaching every now and then for a considerable period of time to come. The teaching of English has not escaped large-scale criticism. While as a compulsory subject of study it stays in the school, it occupies a question of significance in Indian psyche as to whether young people taken through the study of English are found better prepared to manage affairs of life. That pupils have to be more skilful in handling English as a tool for achievement in varied phases of education, goes without saying.

This thought is gaining a firmer conviction among teachers of English also. English is not for the English classroom only; it is for every classroom and for every situation in life. Experts in language teaching were quite convinced that the problem was not one of lack of expertise. "India has an abundance of language teachers. It may be a question of deployment and organisation of this skilled manpower!" We have to think of alternative methods of utilising this expertise. It is admitted that on the pedagogical side, many problems that existed some two decades ago, still continue to exist. Many of them appear to be insoluble. Language teaching is a very difficult task as it involves two aspects—the content element and the skill element. It is true that it is not possible to learn all the latest developments in any field. It is also true that attempting to achieve success and in some cases excellence, is equally motivating and enchanting.

One feels tempted to refer to an article by Charles Newton where he highlights a few facts and figures that indicate the growing importance of English in the modem world and the need for proficiency in this language. Moreover, knowledge of foreign languages is demanded by an increasing number of employers all over the world for the highest paid positions. English is an official language in 63 countries and the mother-tongue of 300 million people. Chinese alone is the mother-tongue of a large number of people—1000 million—but is the official language in only three countries—the People's Republic of China, Taiwan and the Republic of Singapore—and therefore not an official language at the United Nations. He writes, "according to a Gennan analysis made in 1987, Spanish ranks next to English in international importance as the mother-tongue of 280 million people and an official language in 23 countries. Russian is next, as the mother-tongue of 215 million people, but has dwindled in importance as an international language after the collapse of Soviet Union. Since then English and German are gaining importance in the former Communist block countries in Eastern and Central Europe. Hindi is the mother-tongue of 200 million people, but not recognised as an international language, because it is officially used in only one country—India. Indonesian too, is the mother-tongue of 200 million people and therefore ties with Hindi for fifth place. Arabic is the official language in 22 countries, where it is the mother-tongue of 150 million people, and therefore an official language at the United Nations as well. Portuguese too, is the mother-tongue of 150 million people in seven countries and ties with Arabic for sixth place among the world's important languages. Bengali is the mother-tongue of 145 million people and is seventh, only a wee bit behind Arabic and Portuguese. Japanese as the mother-tongue of 115 million people, is eighth; German, mother-tongue of 103 million people is ninth, and French, as the mother-tongue of 68 million people in 24 countries is tenth. According to experts, to what was the Soviet Union, 7000 languages are spoken by 3000 ethnic groups in the world, but according to the Germans, 5000 languages are in use."

Till 1930s, German was the world's most important scientific language, but defeat in two world wars undermined its international prestige considerably. Now it ties with Portuguese as an international language recognised officially in seven countries. In 1910 the German far surpassed English as a scientific language, when it was the mother-tongue of 33.7 per cent of those who were awarded the Nobel Prize in the natural sciences. In 1980, only 11.9 per cent of such scientists claimed German as the mother tongue. Most researchers in Poland, Hungary, France, Netherlands, the USA, Russia and Japan recommend the learning of English. German is recommended by the next largest group of researchers and French holds the third place.

In job advertisements in newspapers, in 1990, in Hungary, Poland, France, Britain, Spain and Italy, where knowledge of foreign language was required, English was the most in demand in all these countries, except in Hungary (where German was more important than English). Next to English and German, knowledge of French and Spanish was in demand (in that order).

In India, although English is a foreign language, it occupies the position of:

(i) An associate official language.

(ii) It is used widely as a link language in offices and among the educated people.

(iii) In such a background English occupies a very important place as a second language in the school curriculum and for higher education. Without exception, every secondary school child has to learn English as a subject, usually for six years but in some cases for three years only.

(iv) English, within the Indian sub-continent, is also, in a great many schools, colleges and universities, used as the medium of instruction.

(v) In the interest of wider communications with the outside world, bilateral, multilateral for purposes—diplomatic, trade and commerce, travel, defence and others, learning of foreign languages is being encouraged. English is being largely used.

(vi) For wider academic, cultural, and scientific interests and utility, English language is greatly used.

Let us see how the situation has taken shape in school and university education. We find specific directions given by Indian Education Commission Report (1964-66). It is stated, a working knowledge of English will be a valuable asset for all students and a reasonable proficiency in the language will be necessary for those who proceed to the university. English will also be used as a 'library language'. The Commission recommends that its teaching may begin in Class V (11+) but it also realised that for many pupils, particularly for rural areas its study will not commence before class VIII (14+). In several Indian states, the teaching of English begins at class III, *i.e.*, when the learner is 8-9 years old. There are many schools primarily convents, public schools and other English-medium schools that start teaching English right from class I.

The specific objectives of teaching and learning English are nonetheless spelt out (VI-VIII) in terms of language abilities of listening, speaking, reading and writing with reference to certain language materials which obviously shall comprise structural or lexical items. A hierarchy of graded competencies from elementary to sophisticated limits have been outlined. The abilities to understand, speak, read and write English are also detailed out therein (NCERT Syllabi, P 29, 1988). For the realisation of the broader objectives, the specification of abilities in a near-micro manner as have been worked out in the syllabus however, prove disjointed, unrelated and thereby somewhat lacking in a major co-ordination of different segments of the skills thereafter. As a result, a fusion of competencies to lead to a cohesive whole—the language experience—is likely to come about. The syllabus has been designed into: *(a)* linguistic content (which shows a more structural rather than communicative schemes of pattern); and *(b)* thematic content (which very much takes off to 'Communicative Approach' contexts, having less regard for structural-situational designed texts). A little elaboration perhaps will be helpful. The syllabus bearing linguistic content reflects two broad divisions, *e.g.*, *(i)* Types of sentences, and *(ii)* grammatical items, the latter gets developed into five important components of grammar. The drilling of grammar separately or integrated in lessons is not acknowledged as beneficial in the scheme of functional counteractive way of learning/teaching English. A great difficulty arises, and that is because of an indecision in adopting either fully structuralists way of learning English or fully communicative way of acquiring English. The second alternative is difficult to feel comfortable with right now, when the country-wide school English syllabus had followed the structural design for more than two decades. This transition period is infested with a lot of confusion, indecision and incompetence both at the stage of planning and execution of English language teaching in the country.

The teaching-learning (English) strategies take cognizance of the process of curriculum transaction in English with regard to development of skills through prescribed texts. If we think along the communicative view, the learner should use the language for expression of ideas, meaning and feeling in addition to using the language for interaction and communication. Therefore, the primary units of language are not merely its grammatical and structural features; but it should comprise some categories of functional and communicative meaning. The present guidelines for syllabi highlight mainly a linguistic and instrumental level, whereas, it should broaden its scope to encompass individual learner's learning needs, a general educational level (learning within the school curriculum), an affective level of interpersonal relationship, and, conduct (expression of values, social graces and conduct etc.), and a content level (various subject disciplines). It will be better to synthesize all cognitive-behavioural-affective co-ordinates into one to facilitate the process of language acquisition. A difficult process indeed. The teaching strategies (in the NCERT guidelines) that have been included into the methodology, go, however, with the communicative principles.

The customary division of language skills into listening, speaking, reading and writing and their treatment as macro-concepts will not serve any purpose. The profile of 'communication needs' for a participant learner cannot stand on such customary division of language skills. Suppose we understand a 'skill' as a micro-concept and an activity' as a macro-concept. The 'skills' lead on to a resultant 'activity'. A learner is reading a piece of prose and trying to understand it; he moves backward and forward following the connectors between a previous statement and a statement that follows. He needs to understand relation between parts of a text through grammatically cohesive device (a language skill) in order to understand the passage (communicative activity). On the basis of the Communicative Needs Processor (John Munby: *Communicative Syllabus Design*, 1986), Munby talks of taxonomy of language skills (p.117): "This taxonomy consists of some two hundred and sixty skills, sub-categorised in fifty-four groups. It is hoped that this organisation will facilitate the process of selecting skills appropriate to previous specified activities." Munby's book outlines these skills into groups in his Chapter, titled, "Language Skills Selection." We admit that we are not yet ready for choosing 'Communicative Approach' in teaching English. Still some states are making a headway for a transit-not complete though—wherein rethinking of structuralists way of developing language skills has resulted in courses that incorporated largely the functional communicative design. For teacher training purpose it proposes a major breakthrough. Preparation of text book materials is a big hurdle.

The primary aim of teaching English in secondary schools in India is to enable the pupils to learn as well as to understand, speak, read and write the English language. These aims are fulfilled within a period of six to seven years of secondary stage starting at the age of 12. The Indian teacher of English needs a sound knowledge of general linguistics which will help him to formulate for himself the relation between language and literature, to find out the essential elements in the learning of English language, to have knowledge of contemporary English and also to study his local variety of English. He has to secure a stable basis for teaching and maintaining a reasonable spoken standard through a study of the phonetics of English. He has to keep abreast with the current trends in English with a view to building up selective and delightful reading material for his pupils.

The context of language policy and language teaching are not being discussed in this chapter as these have been dealt with in the other book '*Teaching of English—A Modern Approach*', by the same author. Instead, a few research studies in this domain can significantly be referred to. One research intended to study the language policy accepted by the government of India in relation to the educational needs and aspirations of different linguistic communities staying in Southern and Northern part of Delhi. The investigator found a significant difference between the two groups belonging to the south and the north linguistic communities of India. Both these groups expressed the desire that the teaching of three languages should not be limited to the lower secondary level, *i.e.*, from Classes VI to VIII; but should be continued till senior secondary level of school education, that is up to Class XII. Further, though both south and north—favoured the learning of Hindi and English as the two compulsory languages, they differed on the issue of the third language to be studied in the school. The south favoured mother tongue with the combination of Hindi and English whereas, the North favoured RL in addition to Hindi and English. Regarding official work of the country, both South and North agreed to the use of English language.

Regarding the medium of instruction, it was noted that the said two groups favoured mother tongue till secondary stage of school education. They further said that at the senior secondary stage, the medium should be English, although the two languages can also be adopted as medium of instruction at the lower secondary and senior secondary levels in schools. In another study the researcher worked on an assessment of the actual working of the languages in the school curriculum in Delhi. One can say that a full-fledged language policy of the government came into operation since seventies. It is admitted that the Three Language Formula as an official language policy of the government of India, its impact on the students, the teachers, and the public might reveal interesting truths about its practice.

The pragmatic ideals far surpass the emotive and ideological milieu that prevailed in early days of independence. As far as linguistic minority schools (different state language) in Delhi are concerned, education at primary and secondary level in mother tongue is a rarity. The schools, by and large, are using either Hindi or English as the medium of instruction. The study of different regional languages are introduced at lower levels only, although there is no bar for a very minority group to study Urdu, Tamil, Gurmukhi and Bengali. English, as an associate official language is being taught as a compulsory second language upto Class X and XII. There is a provision to teach the mother-tongue at the primary level as the minority language schools wish. In practice, Hindi is introduced along with mother tongue at the primary level and adopted as the medium of instruction too. A good number of schools teach English from the primary classes, sometimes introducing English as a medium of instruction even. English as a language is difficult for them, but the mother tongue was neither too easy to learn and use. In spite of this, 73 per cent—a majority indeed—of students expressed their opinion that the learning of the three languages did not constitute a burden for them.

In fact, the first, second and third languages were to be taught compulsorily for ten, six and three years respectively, but the question of 'which' language or languages should be taken up as first, second and third language was left to a very liberal and flexible pattern of language curriculum. Nowhere any compulsion was felt except that a pattern of three languages should be prescribed for the school course for the Indian children and this was, by and large, being found implemented.

Now we turn our eyes on to the language policy at the higher education and therein to look into the position of English language at the post-independent era. It is amazing to know that English as a language was never imposed on the Indians. In fact, Indians themselves wanted it. Initially, the primary objectives must have been placement in jobs and the study of Western Science and Literature, and later on, it spread over different domains and aspects of life. A perusal of the British Parliamentary Papers reveals that English was never introduced first in school system. Studies of English started at higher education level; English got introduced as medium of instruction with the establishment of three universities at Kolkata, Mumbai and Chennai. Later on schools got attached to these universities and encouragement was brought in to introduce English in schools.

The purpose of going into the details of English in India at the higher educational level is very clear. The question of language policy in a country, along with the searching out of the purposes for which the Constitution never erred against retaining English as an associate official language is to be understood before the question of specific objectives for language teaching is outlined. That the English language studies came first at the higher educational level was linked up with the preparation for the job held. Slowly and gradually, learning English had to get started at the school level. Now, all those who attend schools may not go for higher education. Still school must be the harbinger of the development of capacity for use of English, if knowledge of English was expected at the higher educational level. The two stages therefore, as far as studies of English are concerned are interlinked, although the objectives of learning/teaching English at the two levels are distinctly different. One stage influences the other. The lower stage standard should pave the way for the standard at the higher stage. On the contrary, the higher stage expectations should offer the guidelines or goals for achievement at the school stage.

The spread of English studies at the universities initially and later at lower level of education in school, was a landmark in the position of English in India. Since then English with its advantages and benefits seems to have made permanent roots in India. Although Indians themselves desired to learn English and by using it they fought for their freedom, the nationalistic spirit after independence demanded that however useful it might have been, English must be replaced by an Indian language.

A very close examination regarding policy decisions on English as a medium of instruction in higher education on post-independent era—be it of the Central Advisory Board of Education (CABE) or the University Grants Commission (UGC)—revealed the desirability of retaining English in the Indian scene much more than rejecting it or banning it from India. As early as in 1950, in CABE's seventeenth meeting (1950) when Maulana Abul Kalam Azad acted as a Chairman, a consensus was recorded very much in the line of

Dr Radhakrishnan's (University Education Commission) recommendations that the change of medium of instruction from English to a Federal language would be desirable but it should be gradual lest any fall in the standard were entailed. A chronological study of the proceedings of meetings or reports finalised by such policy-making bodies like UGC, CABE and Ministry of Education from 1950 till today, revealed one significant thing beyond doubt, and, that was the idea of dropping English in Indian education system, was finally dispensed with. On the other hand, there were many occasions—through seminars and workshops at UGC level to ensure UGC's firm policy directed to work out ways and means of improving the standard of English.

Today, regional medium for various college courses and universities are gradually being allowed but with a word of caution, and that is, any change from English to regional language should not be hastened. For sciences at post-graduate level and technological and medical fields rarely request for non-English medium of instruction and examination. It seems the question of retention of English got tied up with the problem of maintaining high standards in higher education, although no such study to establish the comparative merit of English vs any Indian language, as a medium, had been carried out as yet. There is no harm in using regional media in education. But the assessment of students' knowledge, of development of their varied abilities, of testing their acquisition of wider perspective in various fields and ultimately, an intense urge to pursue higher echelons of knowledge, get somehow restricted to narrow limits; in that case, the setting up of a national or international standard remain automatically farfetched.

The multiple dimension of English in education had been acknowledged by the policy makers. The use of English as a library language brings forth the great need for developing the standard of English. It is a heavier responsibility to undertake than using English for a mere working knowledge. Dr DS Kothari made an enlightening utterance. He stated that a change of media should not mean, abolishing English. He rather wanted universities to be bilingual. In many multilingual countries, many languages co-exist without hampering the growth of anyone.

A striking information indeed! The school English syllabus in Malayasia does not have one standard syllabus. Each school following its own methods and differences in standard is phenomenal. In some schools ten-year olds cover the same syllabus that is used at college level. The government schools have their own standardized level which is based on the requirement of English language in rural areas. In other words, the minimum standard achievement is prescribed and sheltered by their government schools.

We have to accept one truth. Higher education should cater to a select group of students; no compulsion need to be imposed. The universities ought to maintain their higher standard. The national production, national excellence must be upheld by high standard alone, because the question of intonational comparability comes in. The university student population should comprise those, who by virtue of their ability and attitudes are likely to retain an intense urge, a superior capability to pursue higher studies. Their scholastic enterprise should contribute to higher and better excellencies in academics and in real life. To be able to use a language as a 'library language' needs bigger scope of functioning, a vitality that a student population can acquire by best of efforts. No casual effort in learning English can develop in students the required competence and thereafter the capacity to use it.

Mere school-English cannot prepare an individual for the use of English as the library language. He needs to have some college education in order to use English as a library language. The study of English literature came into vogue as a post-graduate discipline from almost the beginning of this century. The English syllabuses as given in the calenders of Mumbai, Kolkata and Chennai followed copy-courses of British Universities which gave less stress, in those days, on the language but more on Anglo-Saxon literature and philology as instruments of mental discipline. In late thirties and forties, English syllabus included Modem poetry, drama, fiction, history of literature and literary criticism, giving prominence to Browning, Tennyson, Hardy, Shaw and Eliot, Yeats and Landor-trends, before and after. In early sixties, it was American literature that started becoming popular.

A need was felt to reframe two-fold objectives, one, to highlight literature for masters and honours courses and two, to upgrade the English language of students doing courses other than English, as major. The first was 'discipline-oriented', keeping a humanistic cult in view, and the second, 'learner-oriented'. Learners, because of the change of medium of instruction were seen as acquiring a lower language ability in English. They benefited only marginally from teaching by exposure. A new order of thinking came to the field to suit specialisation-oriented courses called ESP (English for Special Purposes). Hence, the syllabuses were changed, objectives were reframed, course content was reorganised—to suit the need of specialisation as well as to aim at acquiring proficiency in English.

The meaning and purpose of course design of ESP will be discussed later. But it was generally accepted that study of English literature should not and cannot be everyman's cup of tea; but English and its linguistic components are likely to benefit the larger sections of the students both in the sector of using it as a 'tool' for library work, as much as in the day-to-day working sphere. In those days, in the early twentieth century, at the level of graduation, study of English used to bring a lot of benefit. (Delhi University was established in 1922): *(i)* in terms of award of scholarships, and *(ii)* or exemption benefit of certain courses or conditions of examination in lieu of English. Today graduate courses offer a compulsory minimum of qualifying English. So more students have to qualify in English which offers a general course of language. It will be interesting to see which sector—the school or the graduate courses—had undergone changes in the framework in our country. Perhaps there has been less scratching of head at the upper and university level of English and more botheration felt for English at the school stage. Whatever be the reasons, there is little doubt that the teachers of English must view the two levels of English teaching as one continuous frame.

In a very recent research conducted in Delhi University, a deliberate probe was made to enlist a fresh and up-to-date reaction of: *(i)* teachers teaching English, and *(ii)* teachers of non-English subjects, on the varied aspects regarding the trends and dimensions of English in higher education in India. The areas covered were:

(1) the purpose of the English paper—narrow and more specific area,

(2) the utility of English paper—broad and general area,

(3) language skills,

(4) objectives,

(5) courses for which English paper is required most,

(6) English, serving as

  (i) medium of instruction,

  (ii) subject of study, and

  (iii) communication,

(7) standard of proficiency in English of students joining the course and the standard at the time of leaving it,

(8) duration of teaching time,

(9) allocation of marks, and

(10) measures needed for maintenance of standards. The teachers reactions recorded 'and spoken were commendable. One fact emerged, and that was, English was taught well but the purposes were not visualised clearly by the teachers in the same manner, nor with the same perspective either. The 'utility' of English is acknowledged by all. We are not going to the details of the research

> except underlining some significant issues. Something continues to go wrong in our higher education sector, where understanding of purposes of teaching/learning English seems to have been kept outside the area of serious discussion. Co-operative planning between teachers and students around the study of English is seldom done. Students are unable to understand why. Policy recommendations are passed by commissions and committees; these are planned from an angle which may be different from what the students need or the teachers want. The learning of English language should be by way of creating essential need for it at every stage of education. So it is necessary for building knowledge and not for building mere status.

English language should be taught as French or German is taught in the university for students who have studied English till Class X and who came from Hindi medium schools. Interest should be inculcated in students for speaking good English. Therefore spoken English should be given due weightage. Language will not be learnt for any useful purpose, if conversation among students is not brought into practice. Writing skill needs wide practice too. Writing for college magazines should be made compulsory—so say teachers, and competition be held in various aspects. Arranging tutorials in efficient manner should motivate learning English in a relevant and meaningful way. Syllabus, in the teachers' opinion at present, appears unrealistic and impractical. People's attitude needs to change. Everybody recognizes the necessity of a good command over this language in one's day-to-day living as also in the specialisation in different subjects. Studying English and considering it a useful language should not be considered 'slave mentality', said the teachers. In fact, language skills have taken a back seat in people's priorities. English as a subject and a medium, is necessary to equip students with the ability to acquire knowledge and to communicate. As a means of communication English is used in jobs, business sector, in trades and marketing in international co-operation and concerns.

Some of the opinions of non-English subject teachers are interesting too. English is a must as a medium of instruction so far as books on science, technology and a number of courses in higher education, are in English. According to this group, English syllabus should be restructured. Instead of literary stalwarts like Shaw and Keats, the text should be made more relevant and interesting, and if possible Indian writings can be included in the text. They say, "we cannot do away with English language. At present we are not able to do any original work in scientific subjects in Indian languages. We have to produce writers and inventors in science. We also have to strengthen the power of expression among our students for the purpose of contributing to the world scientific literature". For strengthening the expression in English, extra classes, additional coaching on basic English, if necessary, should be arranged by the colleges and departments to enhance power of comprehension and expression, the teachers said. To conclude, the teaching of English, on a more practical syllabus, should be made a pleasant and interesting experience both for the teachers and the taught.

❐

4

Methods of Teaching

English has become an important subject in the educational system of India for more than 150 years. During this period in order to teach English, several methods had been used, based on the principles of Greek and Latin grammatical rules. But gradually the needs to evolve new methods and techniques to teach English in India was felt, as these older methods were mainly based on the importance given to grammar, translation, reading or writing, and did not provide enough scope for the spoken aspect of the language, which is essentially the most important feature of learning a new language. The grammar-translation method was the oldest method of teaching English in India. It was a relic of Greek, Latin and Sanskrit teaching which, required mostly memorising of grammatical forms. Equal importance was given to Grammar and Translation. It aimed at teaching English through the mother-tongue, involving a word for word translation. The advocates of this system claimed that it was based on very sound principles. Which are as follows:

1. The structure of foreign 'language can best be learnt when compared and contrasted with that of the mother-tongue. This can best be achieved through translation. This method stressed reading and made little provision for training in speech.
2. Foreign phraseology can best be interpreted through translation.

3. Foreign phrases can be best assimilated during the process of translation.

Advantages

There were several obvious advantages of this method which are described below:

1. Translation helps quicker understanding, avoids vagueness, ensures proper exactness and definiteness.
2. Translation quickens the process of learning, and is hence time-saving.
3. In translation, a very strong bond is established between the native word and the foreign word, thus proceeding from known to unknown.
4. Concrete objects like sea and road can be easily explained which is not possible through imagery and pantomime. Abstract qualities like honesty, loyalty, punctuality etc. can best be understood through direct translation.

In actual practice however, it was soon realised that wholesale translation as a means of teaching a foreign language was futile. Customs and feelings of nations differ greatly. These differences are reflected in the language. There are thousands of words in English that have no exact equivalent in Indian languages *e.g.*, "mist", "lass", "frost" etc. According to Dr Ballard, "To speak any language, whether native or foreign entirely by rule is quite impossible."

Disadvantages

Following are the disadvantages of this method.

1. It completely neglected speech practice—reading and writing came first which is a very unnatural order, in language, learning. It becomes difficult and monotonous. Languages cannot be learnt be learning grammatical rules or dictionary meanings. Language learning is an art and

requires as much practice as any other art. The method was incomplete and difficult.

2. Word-for-word translation destroys fluency of speech and will not be spontaneous. The procedure was very lengthy while this method interfered with cultivating the habit of rapid reading.
3. Exact replicas of foreign words are very often impossible.
4. Unit of reading according to this method was a word, not a sentence. Thus when a child should be assimilating sentences, he is busy in analysing words *i.e.* translating words and phrases into mother-tongue and vice-versa. This could give rise to literal and unidiomatic translation.

DIRECT METHOD OF TEACHING ENGLISH

The Direct Method was adopted for language-teaching by most missionary schools towards the beginning, of the 20th century. The objective of Direct Method was to teach the language directly without help of the mother tongue. It aimed to create a direct bond between the foreign word and its meaning thought and expression. Felix Franke says that the moment a concept (meaning) and foreign word are intimately brought into contact without the intervention of the mother tongue we have the Direct Method.

The Direct Method connects a new word or expression of the child directly with what it stands for, and an attempt is made to minimise the use of mother-tongue. For this the right atmosphere is necessary. Hence, the main aim of this method was to enable the pupils to think in English and use of the foreign language as much as possible. Speech rather than reading received greater emphasis *i.e.* emphasis well on the active side of language learning. It was claimed that fluency in reading and facility in writing naturally follow fluency in speech.

The Direct Method aimed at developing in the pupils that instinctive unerring sense which we possess in our mother-tongue.

This language sense is very essential for acquiring mastery over a new language.

Basic Principles of Direct Method

1. ***Oral Teaching:*** It laid great emphasis on the oral aspect of the language, and there had to be purely oral teaching, in the beginning. An attempt was made to establish a direct bond between expression at every stage. For acthieving this purpose, the best method was to make the pupil constantly hear and speak English.

2. ***Inhibition of the Mother-tongue:*** The use of the mother-tongue had to be reduced to a minimum. No rival sounds were allowed to intervene so that direct associations between experience and expression, word and meaning, in English could be established. When an idea or object is presented to a pupil, he tends to interpret it in terms of his mother-tongue. The Direct Method tried to create an English atmosphere by using English as much as possible and avoiding the use of the mother-tongue, in the class room.

3. ***Inductive Teaching of Grammar:*** Strictly speaking, theoretical grammar had no place at all in the Direct Method, since it implied a system of acquiring a language by actually using it. Thus, the Direct Method did not approve of the teaching of formal grammar nor the memorising of its rules and maxims. This did not however, imply the complete absence of grammar. The method made use of grammar in the sense that the linguistic material was graded grammatically. Grammar was taught inductively. Speaking, reading and writing preceded the teaching of grammar.

4. ***Sentence as Unit of Speech:*** Unlike the Grammar-Translation Method which analysed the foreign language word by word, the Direct Method used sentences as the

expression, for one cannot say anything sensible with knowledge of a mere host of words. It is in sentence that the child learns to talk, or in groups of words that imply sentences.

Advantages

1. Mcnee asserts that this was the quickest way of getting a start with English within a few months, a sound foundation of 500 words can be achieved.
2. This method helped children to think in English, hence their power of self-expression is developed.
3. It called for alertness and activity on the part of both teacher and children.
4. It was based on sound psychological principles and psychological maxims of good teaching.
5. Fluency of speech is increased. With greater stress on oral work, here was great improvement in pronunciation. Because of emphasis on speech, language soon becomes a living activity and not a dead thing.

The weakness of the method becomes apparent in practice. It undermined the significance of written work and reading. Not enough importance was given to reading and written work.

Disadvantages

1. Critics have felt that the very word Direct Method is a misnomer. In the Translation Method, the medium of teaching was the mother-tongue. In Direct Method we use synonyms, images, etc. Hence, it cannot be called direct. Direct association is possible only in a very few cases.
2. Words like "snow" and "mist" could not be introduced effectively through Direct Method for often the explanation becomes more difficult that the original word.

3. This method did not prove to be very successful in India, as it is natural for Indian children to think in their mother tongue.

4. A paucity of good teachers with a fluent command over English also was responsible for the failure of this method to be an effective method for teaching English in Indian schools.

5. It was based on the principle of oral-aural impressions. But this was not effective in all cases for in some children, visual impressions are more strong.

6. Dr West, the greatest critic of this method, stated that great stress on hearing and speaking belittled the importance of reading and writing.

DR WEST'S NEW METHOD OR READING METHOD

Dr West, the innovator of the New Method, believed that by far the greater number of Indian students required only a passive knowledge of English. He observed Indian conditions and concluded that learning to *read effectively* is the shortest method to learning English for Indian children. The reason is that all Indian children have to learn two and three languages and hence the main aim of learning English for Indians is the utilitarian aim. Moreover, how many Indian children have the chance to go abroad? So why burden them with too many technical details of English? Some children are not even able to finish high school. Hence the best thing is to give children the maximum benefit of the language through reading. Reading according to Dr West, is a passive activity whereas talking and writing are active.

Thus Dr West suggested that until about his 12th year, the Indian pupil should be engaged in learning to read English only for the following reasons:

1. Learning to read a foreign language is easy, so the child can begin it early.

2. A reading lesson is not affected by the size of a class for all can read simultaneously.
3. Teaching to read a foreign language is easy so that the-lower grade teacher can undertake it.

To encourage reading, Dr West provided a series of readers containing interesting reading matter with controlled vocabulary. He believed that the child should be able to read with ease and pleasure at the earliest possible stage. He kept the size of the vocabulary small and distributed new words in the lessons evenly to facilitate reading, and understanding. New words when introduced were repeated many times to familiarise the reader. Extensive use was made of pictures and use of the mother tongue was permitted.

A teacher's handbook accompanied every reader with useful hints.

West claimed that "learning to read a language is by far the shortest road to learning, to speak and write it".

Disadvantages

The linguistic material was not presented to any clearly defined grammatical plan. West overestimated the value of passive work as an aid to active work. Oral drill in the use of the language is more helpful in fixing phraseology than silent reading. West's theory that silent reading is a key to speaking and writing is not corroborated by modern investigation into language learning. It is now agreed that the best way to learn a new language is through speech. Learning to read is not the same as learning to speak. We need a vocabulary in both cases, when we speak we use what words we please and a small vocabulary may be adequate to express all our ordinary ideas. But when we read we cannot choose our vocabulary and we have to accept the vocabulary of the writers. Hence, the ideal speaking vocabulary is most easily learnt and most easily used to convey a large number of ideas.

This method was sometimes referred to as the Bi-Lingual Method, as it made use of both, the mother-tongue and English.

West groups words under 2 main classes:

1. Words that we talk *with* or form (structural) words which make up-the form (structure) of the language.

2. Words that we talk *about* or content words which consist largely of nouns.

The new method appealed to teachers first. But its drawbacks were later realised especially the difficulty of completing all the readers in a given time. Vocabulary being graded, it was necessary to complete one set of books before going to the next, hence this method did not prove to be a great success in actual practice, and was soon dropped as a method of teaching English in India.

THE STRUCTURAL APPROACH

Today English is almost a world language. It is the first language of Great Britain, Australia and United States of America. It holds a very important place as a second or third language in India, Pakistan, Sri Lanka, Thailand, Singapore, Hong Kong and many European and South American nations. A great deal of research has been undertaken on the best methods of teaching it as a foreign language by the British Council and several American universities such as Michigan, Cornell and Georgetown. Experiences of language expert have brought to light one very important fact related to language teaching *i.e.*, the teaching-learning should be essentially oral, involving active use of the language in life-like situations. It has been realised that learning a language is like acquiring a skill, like swimming or driving which involves a great deal of practice in actual situations. It is not an intellectual activity involving the learning of vocabulary or grammatical structures.

The Structural Approach does not differ very greatly from the Old Direct Method. In fact, there are a number of similarities between the Direct Method and the New Approach such as the importance of oral world, more pupil activity, inhibition of the mother-tongue and incident of teaching of grammar. The Direct Method has been altered and some additions have been done based on the modern researches of foreign language learning which has resulted in the New Approach. Most teachers feel that it is a different form of the Direct Method, which is true to a very great extent, hence it is often referred to as the New Direct Method.

The Structural Approach is an approach and not a mere method as the older methods of teaching English. The traditional methods guided teachers on how to teach a language *i.e.* the technique of teaching, and paid little or no attention to *what* was to be taught to the student. The New Approach gives clear guidelines on not only how to teach English as a foreign language but also gives detailed instructions on what to teach *i.e.*, the content of the language course. The Structural syllabus consists of 275 structures which have been very carefully graded to a clearly defined grammatical plan, and 2500 to 3000 root words. By the end of six years of learning English, a student is expected to gain a working knowledge of the language whereby he can converse and communicate in simple English and can read and write grammatically correct English of a fairly idiomatic manner.

A structure is either an arrangement of words embodying a grammatical point that conveys a particular meaning, or an inflexion of and word like "ing" added to verbs to make the present continuous tense *e.g.,* "They go to school", and "They are going to school".

Although words on their own are important in language, they cannot be used in isolation. Structural words or the right grouping of words are necessary to convey the right meaning. A structural syllabus concentrates on the correct grading of structures, structural words and content words. It provides the material for teaching English right from the first lesson onwards. Structures may be defined as the tools of a language. Just as a carpenter, blacksmith or goldsmith works with his tools, in much the same way the teaching and learning processes of a language are worked upon by its structures. Each language has its own pattern of structures. So is the case with English. Meaningful words are used in a particular order to convey their meanings.

One of the great advances in the field of linguistic science is the discovery that the word is much less important than the way which words are put together. One may know 500 words of a foreign language, but unless one can put them together in a meaningful sentence, they are of no use at all. Vocabulary thus assumes a secondary, though still important position, while the structural pattern is really important and a fundamental thing. A structural syllabus concentrates on the handling of "structural words". What we mean is words such as prepositions, pronouns, auxiliary verbs, conjunctions and some adverbs, which form the skeleton of the language, while the flesh, and blood is provided, by the content words to nouns, verbs, adjectives and most adverbs. Structural words are the most important words in a language, but they are also the most difficult to learn and use correctly. Thus a thorough drilling of the structural patterns will overcome the drawbacks of grammatical difficulties and lack of incentive.

A careful study of English language, experimental investigation and research have brought to light that there are 275 language patterns which constitute the core of essential english. These are the structures in which *each embodies an important grammatical point*. These structures are carefully graded so that the cumulative approach will give the young learner a working command of spoken and written English at the end of the course.

In grading structures, attention is paid to *both meaning and form*. Only one meaning of a word is taught at a time and is established by practice before another meaning is taught. Each meaning is taught as a fresh item.

PRINCIPLES FOR GRADING STRUCTURES

(1) **Usefulness:** For our purpose this means practicability and frequency. All the structures of the language are not equally useful, for some occur more frequently than others. Thus, those structures may be more useful which occur frequently in the spoken and written language. Those are also useful which help in the

building up of the language (*e.g.* Use of "such", "as", "must", "ought", "request").

(2) **Productivity:** Ideally, one structure should lead on naturally to the next so that the complete syllabus becomes a series of interlocking items, *e.g.,* "I am giving this book" to "He is taking this book."

(3) **Teachability:** This implies that a structure is more teachable-than another *e.g.,* "We are opening the book" is more teachable than "Rajesh comes late everyday". The former can be taught more easily, by really opening the book. Structures that can be easily demonstrated in a realistic situation are better to teach.

(4) **Simplicity:** Simplicity is also an important feature, simplicity in form and meaning to follow the maxim—Proceed from simple to complex.

PRINCIPLES OF THE STRUCTURAL APPROACH

Foreign language teaching should prescribe to the following principles:

1. The approach should be primarily *oral.*
2. Active methods of teaching should be used as far as possible. Students activity should receive more attention.
3. The greatest possible use of the foreign language should be made in the classroom.
4. Teaching of the language should be done more as the imparting of a skill rather than as the provision of information about the form of the language.
5. Careful grading should be done of pronunciation, vocabulary and grammar for presentation.

According to this approach and modern researches, properly graded structures are as important and indispensable to the modern language teacher as properly graded vocabulary. The optimum period of time needed to teach a foreign language in a normal school system should be 6 hours a week for 6 school years (one period daily from fifth onwards).

MAJOR CHARACTERISTICS OF STRUCTURAL APPROACH

The main charateristics of this approach are:

1. **Oral Work:** Foreign language teachers all over the world agree that the oral method of teaching is the best method for both children and adults alike. Language is obviously speech before it is anything else. In fact, writing is only speaking with the fingers and reading is only listening with the eyes. Every structure should hence be taught and drilled orally first. Thus oral work is the cornerstone of the new approach. Through speech the pupil learns to make a direct connection between the English word or phrase and its meaning and acquires the habit of using words in correct sentence patterns.

Many of the common errors of children are due to the teacher's emphasis on reading and the reader with not enough speech.

The six processes involved in the study of a language are:

(a) Recognise and understand the spoken foreign work.

(b) Pronounce by imitation the foreign word.

(c) Use the foreign word correctly *i.e.* oral and written composition.

(d) Understand the foreign written word without learning it *e.g.*, in silent reading.

(e) Recognise and pronounce (1 +2) the written foreign word *e.g.*, in oral reading.

(f) Write the foreign word.

The number of these processes can be effectively lessened by starting with oral work. Speaking and listening should always precede reading because learning a language is largely a matter of right habits. These are established only by practice and frequent repetitions.

Thus the teaching of English starts with oral work. During the first 6-8 weeks, regular reading and writing are not practised. These may be incidental to relieve the monotony of oral work. Oral practice is the quickest way of making a start. In order to read, the student has to learn to connect with each symbol or set of symbols and its corresponding sounds, *e.g.*, b-a-t = bat.

However, in order to write, he has to learn first how to make written symbols which is a laborious process. But in speech he has merely to imitate the words and sentence patterns of others, and he soon gets going. This has a valuable psychological effect on him. It supplies a stimulus and an interest in further learning which is taking where the sense of progress is not present. It is a fact that to be able to speak a language makes that language learning more real to the pupils than to be able to read and write it only. The oral-aural appeals stronger than the visual. In acquiring a foreign language, the pupil feels the language to be real, vital and useful and therefore interesting as he learns to use it, in speaking about things that most often touch his life and come into his mind.

2. **Children's Activity:** Because language is learnt mainly through use and language becomes more meaningful when it is accompanied by activity, hence a great deal of emphasis is laid on child-activity in the approach. Pleasurable activity is the secret of success in language assimilation. In our secondary school classrooms we need more group-work, projects, handwork, language games, story-telling by children, dialogues and plays, drawing and colouring, correcting dictations written by children, writing on the BB and such similar activities. According to Palmar, listening is an activity of the adult life, when rest and concentration have been developed and when rest and repose are pleasant. But in childhood, movement and a constant lifting of attention is habitual and largely unconscious. In teaching young children therefore, listening should be followed

by action that reveals whether understanding has taken place. The action need not necessarily be actual bodily action, though for young people that is the best. It may be putting a clasp or a tick opposite a picture, painting picture, jumping, skipping etc. Sentences are recited and acted out the same time.

Gouin says—"It is not only the spoken language, but the action with it that is the secret of learning a language."

This is both biologically and psychologically true. Thus language action is both meaningful and purposeful. Everyone uses action reinforce meaning—gesture with hands, eyes, head or expressions because we feel that it requires emphasis and movement to make the meaning clear. Hence for young children, nearly all sentences should be accompanied by action. This harnessing of speech and action may also be graded—mime, dialogues, dramatic activity, story-telling, acting etc. A further value to this is that it arrests the interest and activity of the pupils. Learning becomes more complete and thorough and greater attention is paid to pronunciation which is otherwise neglected.

Because the Structural Approach stimulates greater student activity and interest, it is known as *English through playway*. This method can be used right from the beginning of the new language-learning such as nursery rhymes with action, more so when set to music, dramatic activity etc.

3. **Inhibition of the Mother tongue:** The Structural Approach discourages the use of the mother-tongue or translation, in the teaching of English, as translation creates an obstacle in the process of forming correct language habits. It also slows down the speed of grasping correct English. An important point to remember is that no structure should be translated into the mother-tongue, and no teaching point should be brought directly to the pupil's notice. New words should be introduced through activity, pictures, etc. It is not proper to give the vernacular equivalents of words, as this weakens the impression which the word makes on the mind and of pupils' curiosity slackens.

However, when all devices fall, slight use of the mother-tongue may be made to convey the proper meaning, but the teacher should revert immediately to English.

The use of the mother tongue should be made judiciously under the following circumstances:

(a) For explaining abstract words like honesty, produce, antiquity etc. to save time.

(b) For giving instructions.

(c) For quick and short testing.

(d) For bringing out any grammatical point to the students notice.

DIFFERENCE BETWEEN OLD METHODS AND STRUCTURAL APPROACH

The Structural Approach has several differences, when compared with the traditional method of teaching english:

1. Grammar is neither a separate subject in New Approach as it was in the old Grammar Translation Method, nor is undue emphasis given to grammar teaching in the English teaching course.

2. The New Approach makes careful grading of Tenses. The earlier readers made use of the Present Continuous Tense, and gradually the simple. Present and Past Tense are introduced. This is unlike the Direct Method in which the Past Perfect Tense and the Passive Voice were used even in the first book.

3. Vocabulary in the Structural Approach is fixed at 3000 root words with its derivatives and collocations. This is unlike the older Direct Method which had no control over the introduction of vocabulary at any stage, irrespective of the age or experience of the learners.

4. In the Direct Method, selections from good writings of English, literature were included in the readers. The New Approach has prose lessons specially written for the readers, keeping in view the age and standard of the students according to a well-graded structural plan.

5. The New Approach, requires a very lively, enthusiastic and resourceful teacher, who will think of various ways in which to keep the learners busy and interested, unlike the older methods in which passive and dull teachers continued to teach English to over-populated classrooms.

6. Older methods entailed greater teaching activity. In the New Approach the emphasis of activity shifts from the teacher to the students, making the learners active participants in the teaching-learning process.

SIMILARITIES WITH OLD METHODS

1. The Structural Approach is primarily oral in its approach and in this respect it has a great deal of similarity with the Direct Method. In fact, this is one of the respond why the Structural Approach has often been called the New Direct Method. An initial teaching has to be done orally, and a lot of emphasis is laid on speech to make language learning a living experience and not a dull bookish activity.

2. The reader of the Structural syllabus is always accompanied by a teacher's handbook. In this respect, it is similar to Dr West's New Method, which made plentiful use of teacher's handbooks, workbooks, companion and composition books, and supplementary readers.

3. In the importance given to drill work, different types of vocabulary and graded and systemic books, the Structural Approach is similar to Dr West's New Method. The New Approach however, has made the introduction of controlled vocabulary and structures more organised and systematic.

DEFINITE IMPROVEMENTS OF THE STRUCTURAL APPROACH

The New Approach has certain advantages over the older methods. Being the result of widespread researches in language teaching, Structural Approach embodies certain distinct and obvious improvements over the older methods:

1. It has made the teaching of English more definite and systematic. The Approach involves the mastery of 275 basic English structures and 3000 root words taught according to well-organised plan of teaching that is primarily oral.

2. It has fully integrated grammar and composition teaching. Grammar is not an end in itself but serves as useful aid to composition, which is essentially the ability to communicate effectively, whether oral or written.

3. The lessons are graded grammatically. The readers of the structural syllabus start with the Present Continuous Tense and then introduce the Past, Future and Simple Present Tense successively to avoid confusion. Structures are graded keeping in view the age, ability and past experience of the learners, and introduction of vocabulary too is carefully controlled into working vocabulary and of recognition vocabulary.

4. Special lessons have been written in prose based on well-known standard works of English Literature, or the interests of learners. These lessons embody a few structures and have controlled vocabulary. Only a few new words are introduced in each lession and repeated for a few times in the succeeding lesson.

5. The main emphasis of the New Approach is on pupil activity. In fact the pupils are kept busy all the time, either repeating after the teacher, doing some actions, solving puzzles or singing. The activity has to be pleasu-

rable most of the time, making the language learning almost a game. Hence, the approach is often called "English through Playway."

6. The Structural Approach makes great demands on the teacher. The teacher has to evolve original and noval methods to keep the students active and interested all the time, while keeping himself in the background. The widespread use of situations and experiences of the pupils requires all the resourcefulness of the teacher. Moreover, the teacher must have a perfect command over the English language to make language-learning an exhilirating experience.

7. The Structural Approach presents a well-organized plan of teaching English to the teacher, with detailed instructions not only on how to teach English, but also on what to teach.

8. The New Approach insists on active learners. The pupil is keen and attentive all the time, keeping in view the belief that it is only in activity that a person learns. The Approach frowns on the passivity of learners according to the older methods of teaching. This greater pupil activity make this approach psychologically superior to the earlier methods. When children are able to speak or write a few sentences in English even during the first year of the English course, this provides a great deal of sense of satisfaction to the pupils, providing the necessary psychological motivation for the urge to learn more.

❑

5

Learning of English Language

Learning a new language is like learning a new skill. This cannot be done through lectures such as learning history or science but through plenty of practice in the actual situation such as learning to swim or to ride a bicycle. Thus learning a language must be done through plenty of practice of listening, speaking reading and writing. This is often forgotten resulting in bookish and unidiomatic language learning.

Processes of Language Learning

Learning a foreign language involves the following processes:

(a) Learning the sound system of the language.

(b) Learning the basic sentence pattern language.

(c) Learning the vocabulary suited to his needs.

(a) **Speech Sounds:** Learning a new language means mastering its sound system, by producing correctly all the sounds in isolation and in combination. The learner should employ in his speech the international patterns of the foreign language so as to be intelligible to its natives. Native sounds should not intervene in foreign sounds.

(b) Vocabulary should be suited to the daily requirements of the learner. It is pointless learning exotic and flamboyant new words which will not be put into practice. A simple and useful vocabulary is more important than a literary one.

(c) **Sentence and Phrase Structure:** Mastering a foreign language means acquiring its most important part *i.e.* sentence, phrase and idiomatic patterns. This becomes a matter of habit, *e.g.* he does not have to think whether to put the object before or after the verb.

LEARNING A FOREIGN LANGUAGE

In learning a foreign language, the process does not involve learning of a long list of words in vocabulary, but it is a three-fold process:

(1) Sound System: The learner must master the sound system and be able to understand the stream of speech, in order to hear the distinctive sound features and to be able to produce them as far as possible exactly.

(2) Vocabulary: The process of putting into use particular structures with some vocabulary items to represent a sound system with meaning is also necessary.

(3) Structure: The learner is required to master the features of arrangement that constitute the structure of the language. These are the matters that the native speaker as a child has acquired early in life as unconscious habits. A new learner has to learn these structures.

It amounts to learning the four basic language skills of understanding, speaking, reading and writing in that order. These have been turned by FG French as follows:

(1) We try to give the pupil the ability to speak English within a limited vocabulary and correctly within the most useful sentence patterns. Speech is essential because language is a spoken thing. For every word than is written or read, millions of words are spoken, writing and printing are only speech reduced to black signs.

(2) We try to give the pupil the ability to understand what is spoken. This is a wider task that the first for it brings

into use a wider vocabulary and all those extra words which are not remembered for immediate use. It also has an obvious practical value. A learner is who says, "Please speak more slowly" has not been taught to listen.

(3) We try to give the pupil the ability to read. This means a great increase in the number of words which are known when seen but which are not ready for immediate use in speech. Reading includes speech and much more.

(4) We try to give the pupil ability to write. This is the hardest task of all and for many learners the least important. To speech, listening and reading it adds spelling, handwriting and punctuation. These four skills are also known as reception and expression.

Reception consists of listening.

Expression constitutes:

(a) Speech

(b) Reading

(c) Writing

Psychological Methods of Learning a Language

The acquisition of language by a child is a very natural process. It does not require any systematic study nor is it a complex intellectual activity. Children instinctively imitate whatever sounds and actions they hear and see in their environment with the result that with maturation and physical growth, children effortlessly pick up their mother-tongue, and even two to three other languages spoken in their environment. This is done without exercising any apparent effort, and as naturally as a child learns to walk and sit. Detailed observations and psychological studies have shown that acquiring a language is akin to acquiring other skills such as cycling or swimming and can be done quite effortlessly if it is approached in the right manner. This is evident from the fact that children have learnt to speak grammatically correct sentences by the age of four to five years, long before they have attempted any formal study of grammar. Also, they have learnt to use the correct forms of the language without receiving any formal training in this. Acquiring mastery over a second or third language can be done with greater ease if the processes involved in acquiring the first language are followed. Some of the psychological processes involved in language acquisition, are learning by imitation and whole method, learning by transfer of training and verbal learning through concept formation.

Learning a language is not an intellectual activity. Every child instinctively learns to imitate what he hears. It is quite a common practice to compare the early utterances of a young child to the imitation sounds of a parrot. Every language is a complex collection of sounds which seem confusing initially. But slowly, as the child listens to it more and more, these complex sounds begin to acquire a meaning. A child's first experience with a language consist of listening and understanding. Comprehension involves the hearing of the distinct sounds that go to make up a language. The next step is the reproduction of these sounds at first incoherently, and then correctly. Initially a child reproduces merely words. It has its own peculiar vocabulary for its favourite things—its bottle, its mother, father, its toys etc. Little by little, it picks meaningful words. By the age of two to three years, the child begins to string two and more words together, so that meaningful words give rise to meaningful phrases and sentences, so that the child has learnt to communicate its basic needs.

The whole process takes place through imitation. Along with imitation, the child also learns by a process of trial and error. The child learns to form a bond of association between a situation and its right response. Through practice and effects of either satisfaction and dissatisfaction, a child learns to attach a meaning to the various words and phrases he hears around him.

Acquiring a new language becomes a pleasant activity involving a satisfying sense of achievement when it attempted as one intelligible whole, and not analysed into its various components of words and their relevant meanings. The Gestalt psychlogists believed that all knowledge should be presented as an organised whole with its components adequately to give the learner an idea of the complete "whole". The view of language learning has been responsible for the fading away of traditional methods of teaching involving long translations and formal grammar teaching and the introducing of methods involving actual use of the language in meaningful context and situation.

Teaching through imitation can be done in classroom situations through teaching of dialogues. The first step is to let students hear the teacher, and then to repeat it as soon as they can. Sometimes, a sentence has to be repeated several times to enable children to get the right structure pattern. Imitation can be started with group or choral recitation, as often shy and inarticulate children hate to repeat on their own. Group repetitions offer clear advantages for drill work to a class of beginners. The student is less inhibited, in a group response, he recites more readily and everyone has a chance to practise every sentence. The pace must however be kept brisk and lively at all times to prevent boredom setting in, which is the greatest enemy of language drill work.

Learning Language Through Transfer of Training

The theory of transfer of training has certain useful applications for language learning, particularly in the case of older and more mature learners. Transfer involves the conscious applications of maxims and experiences of one situation to another situation. Thus, the rules of transfer can be helpful to a learner in comparing and analysing the learning of two languages. It is also helpful in applying the rules and maxims of the learner's first language to acquisition of second and third language.

The most popular exponent of transfer of training was EL Thorndike whose theory of Identical Elements, stated that transfer was possible from one situation to another to the extent that the same elements or components are sound in different situations. These identical elements may be in the form of content or technique.

1. Similarity of Content: The knowledge of one language can help a learner to acquire another language more easily if there are similar components in the two languages such as vocabulary or grammatical constructions. Thus person knowing French can learn English with greater ease as there is a great deal of similarity between the two languages.

2. Similarity of Technique: Knowledge of badminton can help a person to learn tennis with greater ease as the rules and skill governing both the games are similar. In language learning, if a pupil learns that "pre" means before in some works like "preview" and "predict" he can apply the same principle to understanding new words such as "pre-heat" and "predetermine."

Transfer may give rise to interference in many cases. In India, pronunciation of English words generally suffers from interference of the native languages. A conscious study of such interference can help to eliminate the effects of such negative transfer. Transfer depends a great deal on the learner's mental ability and maturity. Transfer is most useful in language learning when a conscious effort to point out similarities and dissimilarities in two languages is attempted. This is especially true in the learning of meaning and basic structures. Thus, it is attained through conscious effort and is not automatic.

Language Learning by Concept Formation

Thinking, reasoning and imagination are all forms of higher thought processes which make use of image, percept and concepts. No thinking is possible unless an individual has some mental pictures or ideas about the things he wishes to express *e.g.* in the statement:

"Sarita attends a co-educational school." The meaning cannot become clear unless a person has some idea of what a school is and what co-education implies. Thus, communication through language is impossible in the absence of a general idea of what the words used stand for. This general idea is a concept. A concept is hence, a memory image of what a thing is. It is not a single image, but a sum total of what a thing stands for, how it looks, smells, sounds etc. Concepts are the result of past experiences and are built up through the senses and percepts. A sensory image with a meaning attached to it gives rise to a percept, *e.g.* a red light at a traffic junction immediately means "stop" without any detailed process of explanation. Concepts are formed through the processes of abstraction and generalisation.

1. **Abstraction:** All knowledge is gained by an individual through one or more of his five senses of seeing, hearing, smelling, tasting and touching. When a child first sees a dog, he may not know what it is. His mother may point out to him that it is a dog. Over a period of several days, he may come across several dogs, and learn to observe the differences and similarities between the animals, so that gradually a mental picture of what a "dog" is forms in the child's mind. Only the essential qualities remain, the unnecessary details of different types of dogs are ignored. This process of analysis whereby a general mental picture of the main qualities which make an animal a dog is known as abstraction.

2. **Generalisation:** When the quality abstracted through experience is applied to a new situation, the process of concept formation is complete *e.g.* if a child who has got a general idea of what a dog is on the basis of various small dogs he has seen in his neighbourhood, is shown a huge "alsatian" which he correctly recognizes as a dog, then he has been able to correctly apply the mental picture he acquired through abstraction, to a novel situation. This is the stage of synthesising past experiences into generalisation and practical application of knowledge.

Many times, this stage is not completed in children, leaving gaps in knowlege, with the result that a horse is mistaken for a donkey. Concepts can be of concrete things, abstract qualities or of relationships. Concepts are not static, but keep on changing on the basis of experiences. Concepts are personal *e.g.* what a rose means to one person may not mean the same to another. To one it may convey beauty, to another it may stand for thorns.

Importance of Motivation and Interest

Education today is not merely the imparting of knowledge, hence to teach effectively, it is vital for the teacher to take into consideration the psychological needs and interests of the learner. It is rightly pointed out that to teach John Latin, the teacher must know Latin and John himself.

HE Palmer, a leading British specialist in the theory and practice of teaching English as a foreign language, in his well-known book "*The Principles of Language Study*", has formulated certain principles of learning a language based on the psychological needs of an individual. These principles can be applied to the teaching of English in India quite effectively. Palmer states that for any language acquisition, there should be interest in the activity, which provides the person with adequate motivation for learning the language. There should be a great deal of initial imitation followed by oral repetition and practice.

Language learning is not an inborn or inherent ability, nor is it an inherited trade. It is an acquired skill that depends upon adequate exposure to the language in the right environment. As English is a foreign language to most Indians, it must be ensured that the learner is given plenty of exposure to the language and opportunities should be given to listen, imitate and then produce the new sounds of the language.

Importance of Concepts in Language

Concepts are very important for learning any language. Language is the symbolic vehicle of thought and no communication is possible unless concepts of various things are built up. In fact, concepts and language are interdependent. There can be no language without concepts and concepts cannot be formed without the use of language. Through the proper use of language concepts are developed, enriched and communicated. The richer and more varied the concepts, the more vivid will be the language. Vocabulary is the means through which concepts are verbalised. Hence a richer vocabulary helps in building more concepts and more effective language. Piaget regarded language as the symbolic vehicle by which thought is carried. The aim of the teacher must be to start the building up of language at the perceptual level where things can be seen, heard or felt. But this is a lower level of thought. Gradually the learner should be raised to the conceptual use of language for thinking and higher thought process such as reasoning and problem-solving. Thus, direct experience should lead to abstract concepts and a rich and varied vocabulary, which is essential for effective language learning.

In India, English has an important place in the educational set-up. In some schools, English is the medium of instruction and thus occupies the pride of place as the first language. In some schools, it is taught as a second or third language. In any case, English is a foreign language to Indians, and hence the teaching of English must be handled with the greatest of care. To achieve thoroughness and economy of effort all teaching-learning must be based on psychological principles of language learning.

LANGUAGE LEARNING—ACQUIRING OF A SKILL

Learning a new language is done with the greatest of ease by small children in any part of the world, and this is quite obvious from the ease with which children pick up their mother tongue. Normally this happens around the age of two to three years with almost no conscious teaching by the parents, and long before children start their formal education. They may remain illiterate, but they will still have an adequate command of the spoken language for all practical purposes. We might compare this 'easy' process of learning to speak with the process of learning to walk. Indeed, the two things seem to begin to develop side by side, with the early growth of both mental and physical faculties.

One important fact that emerges from this is that learning a language is not difficult for a child as it is not, an "intellectual" activity in the sense like learning Arithmetic or Physics. It is far more a development of some innate skill which every, human being is equipped to perform. By contrast, we can observe that no other kind of animal is adopted to performing this function.

The only "training" that the child requires is that of being talked to or even of being present when other people are talking amongst themselves. With this very slight assistance, the child can automatically begin to reproduce the complex collection of sounds made around him, at first only individual words, then in groups of two or three words and finally in full sentences. Another important fact about language is that a child is not born with the skill of speaking and hence it is not one of his innate tendencies. He does have to learn it after he is born, given the right environment. A Scottish scholar once believed that if he isolated a new-born baby where it could not hear its mother-tongue, it would automatically begin to speak it, in a short time. He was proved wrong as the child just continued to make meaningless noises like a six-month old, even after the age of two when any normal child has began to speak quite a lot.

The skill of speaking a language thus is transmitted from generation to generation. A child can learn to speak any language, if he is given the right kind of exposure to it. No language is intrinsically

more or less difficult to learn as a first language than any other. Also each language has the same potential range of expression. Thus language or Sanskrit are in no way more difficult or easy than the more spoken language, like English or Hindi. What language the child will pick up depends entirely on what language he is exposed to since birth and through his formative years. All languages are made up of a selection of all the sounds which human vocal organs can produce, thus.

Different languages can be described as the selection of different sounds in the manner of overlapping circles showing overlapping sounds.

The actual combination of sounds may differ considerably or may be similar, as also the word structure or grammar and syntax. Thus it is child's play for a youngster to pick up one language, and also two or three other languages belonging to the same language family. Moreover, the human brain is especially adopted to mastering these systems of structures and can easily recognize the underlying patterns as belonging to one specific language or another.

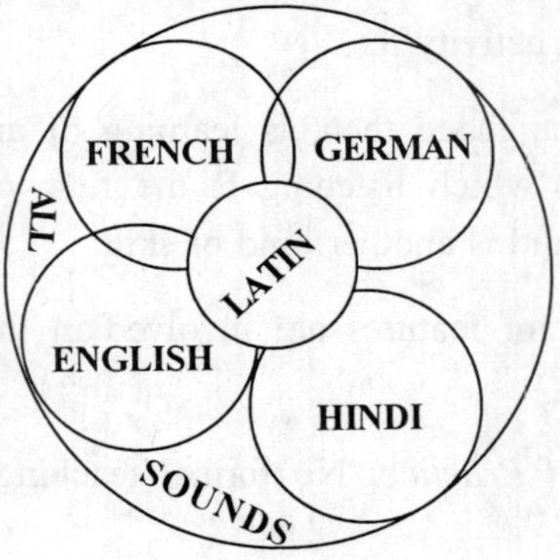

THREE FEATURES OF LANGUAGE LEARNING

The first important feature of the process of learning a language is the quantity of language material that a growing baby is exposed to. Almost every waking hour is spent in verbal give and take. At first, the baby produces very few sounds, most of the time it is merely passive listening.

What the baby is learning to do is very important, to listen when talking about learning, we so often refer to speaking a language to the extent of forgetting, the necessity of listening first. Like all machines, there has to be an input to give some output. A child's capacity to understand far exceeds his capacity to speak. This is true of the mother tongue and even of foreign language learning. Listening involves the reception of different sounds and the conversion thereby the brain into meanings.

This does not require any thought or conscious effort on the part of the listener. No intellectual effort is needed to cope with the concepts. Hence, it is artificial to separate 'understanding' from listening. This automatic process of listening can be compared with other human functions such as learning to use a pencil, learning to eat food, etc. Every growing child can learn these with a certain amount of guidance, and practice. Hence, learning a language is referred to as acquiring of skill like swimming or walking rather than an intellectual activity.

Learning a language then, is learning of an interconnected group of skills of which listening is the first. Speaking always follows listening, and is another kind of skill.

Some important features are involved in the acquisition of language:

1. *Amount of Practice:* No formal teaching but practice is important.

2. Motivation is responsible for the baby's earlier utterances illustrating a desire for contact.

3. *Learning in a Situation:* Environment is important for comprehension.

4. Factors important for initiating language are: Amount of exposure, to language, in situations that illustrate its meaning and motivation to use the language for urgent communication.

PRINCIPLES OF LANGUAGE STUDY

HE Palmer in his famous book, "*The Principles of Language Study*" puts forth the following nine principles involved in the study of any language. According to HE Palmer, language learning is an art. It does not involve much of reading and writing at the initial stages but of understanding what is said, and expressing that we wish to say by speaking.

1. **Initial Preparation:** The purpose of the teacher is to awaken and develop the student, natural and spontaneous capacity for language study, since language learning is an art and not a science. It is the ability to acquire the capacity for doing rather than knowledge. Thus the first attempts at language study have to be imitative which may often be incorrect imitation.

When we may wish to produce a foreign sound just and, we may actually produce a native sound to which we are commed, *e.g.*, *f* and *v* sounds in English are different from native Indian sounds. Similarly we may wish to say a sentence in a foreign language, but we may construct it incorrectly due to the different word order. In English for *e.g.,* the word order is S-O-V while most Indian languages follow the S-O-V pattern. Or we may wish to express an idea and may fail to hit upon the right word. For this plenty of practice in required and this practice is learning through trial and error method of learning. Some efforts are successful and others are unsuccessful, and in the course of practice we gradually eliminate unsuccessful attempts and repeat and strengthen successful ones.

It is also often by making mistakes that we learn, for unsuccessful attempts give way to successful attempts. Language learning is essentially a habit-forming process during which we must acquire new habits. It is a case where often we cannot proceed from known to the unknown, but plunge headlong into the new and unknown.

2. **Accuracy:** No form of work should be adopted which may lead to inaccurate habits of language, for habit-forming without accuracy means the forming of bad habits. Accuracy is too a relative term and implies conformity with a given standard or model. *e.g.*, pronunciation according to BBC standards.

Accuracy may refer to:

(a) Accuracy in sounds.

(b) Accuracy in use of stress and intonation.

(c) Accuracy in spellings.

(d) Accuracy in fluency, *e.g.*, speech of foreigners.

(e) Accuracy in meanings.

(f) Accuracy in combination words.

3. **Habit-forming:** The teacher will not only assist the student in utilising his previously formed habits, but will also cause him to acquire new ones appropriate to the work he is to perform. Thus proficiency in the use of the language must be aimed at. Adult students in general dislike forming new habits and avoid such work as far as possible. They try to study language through discrimination and other processes of the intellect, which are really ineffective so far as language learning is concerned.

4. **Gradation:** This means passing from the known to the unknown by easy stages, each of the which serves as a preparation for the next *e.g.*, structures and vocabulary can be graded as also grammar and syntax.

The gradation can be rationally applied in the following manner:

(a) ***Ears before Eyes:*** All fresh language material should be presented in its oral form and not in its written from. Sound should first be practised without any reference to any written or any graphic forms of representation; the ear not the eye is the organ provided by nature for

recognising and assimilating sounds. Words should first be heard and imitated orally, because ideal assimilation is not helped but hindered when the written form is presented. Fresh word groups and sentences should also as far as possible be first introduced and learnt orally. Adult students find this difficult.

(b) ***Immediate Memory before Prolonged Memory:*** When the teacher should make students repeat immediately after her the new sounds instead of postponing it to the next day.

(c) ***Receipting before Production:*** A student will be unable to reproduce a sound as word until he has really heard the right model. Thus a student should not only be trained to hear, but should be given plenty of opportunity for this.

(d) ***Oral Reception before Reading:*** This will involve imitation of spoken sounds before formal reading is attempted.

(e) ***Drill-work before Free Work:*** This is the most important of precepts to be followed. Drill work should be varied. Firstly, it should involve listening only to perceive and discriminate new sounds, then imitation and articulation and finally exercises to aim at fluency and accuracy of producing new sounds.

(f) ***Chorus Work before Individual Work:*** To avoid embarrassment and laughter of his fellow pupils. Only when a certain mastery has been achieved in group articulations to give a certain degree of confidence, that individual reproductions should be done.

5. **Proportion:** The various aspects of language, *i.e.* understanding, speaking, reading and writing and other aspects such as grammar, syntax and phonetics must receive appropriate attention. Proportion must be observed in deciding the right amount of drill-work and free work, translation and "direct" work, intensive and

extensive reading, of chorus-work and individual work, which is the teacher.

6. **Concreteness:** The student should proceed from concrete to abstract, which is fully illustrated by saying: "Example is better than precept" *e.g.* actually using a new structure is more useful than studying, the rules responsible for the structure, such as the study of direct and indirect speech. Actual use of the direct and indirect forms of speech must be drilled in an appropriate situation rather than giving pupils a list of rules governing the structures.

7. **Multiple Line Approach:** Language study should be approached simultaneously from many different starting points towards one and the same goal *i.e.* proficiency in using the language. Use should be made of each and every method. Different types of exercises, drill-work and devices should be used to bring the learner nearer his goal. The multiple line approach embodies the eclectic principle in its, general and favourable sense to help the teacher in judiciously selecting without prejudice, all type of work that will be helpful in acquiring English as a working language for daily use or for further academic study.

8. **Order of Progression:** The student should first be taught to hear and articulate correctly, then to use previously learnt sentences, then to make sentences on the basis of simple vocabulary so that progress is rapid and results are permanent. Right from the beginning, a rapid and fluent style of pronunciation must be taught to ensure psychological satisfaction at the earliest stages.

9. **Interest:** The methods to be used for language study should be devised in such a way that the interest of the student is always secured. This can be achieved by giving a sense of progress achieved, competition, games, right relation between student and the teachers. Providing a variety of activities to promote interest in language-learning go a long way paving the road for acquiring right language habits and skills.

❐

6

Language Content and Kinds of Lessons

The Structure of English and Kinds of Lessons

It is not required that every English teacher should be a linguist or a psychologist. At the same time, more is expected of the teacher than of any other professional as his is a characteristic vocation. Mostly the English teacher undertakes to teach a lesson without fully knowing the implications the lesson has on the learner's language acquisition as well as without knowing what specific aspects of the language content he wants the pupils to acquire. Every lesson in English has specific relations to some aspect of the content of the language, or rather as we shall be examining in detail, every aspect of English as a language is capable of yielding a specific kind of lesson within the overall framework of language learning. In present-day circumstances with all the emphasis put on the written form of language we no longer need to consider language as exclusively speech. An analysis of the structure of language would yield a variety of elements which usually form part of a course in linguistics. Before anything else is undertaken, it is worthwhile to keep in mind that it is a language as such that the teacher helps the learners acquire, not any of its sub-systems in particular. At the same time, the teaching of the language in a classroom would mean a diversification of its subsystems for purposes of functional convenience and more effective teaching.

English language, consequently is a system which consists of the following sub-components:

(1) Language is *Competence and Performance*. Competence is the 'built-in ability' of the native speaker which forms the 'theoretical base' of the functional-shoots: listening, speaking, reading and writing, all of which involve the actual exercise of the linguistic competence. The actual exercise of the language by means of the four skills, we call, performance. In other words we may identify the performance of English with the exercise of the four language skills.

(2) Linguistic performance would mean, again, two things: Speech and writing, which in terms of language content yield spoken language and written language. Spoken language, in turn, apparently consists of sounds and meanings, while written language consists of graphemes and meanings.

(3) The knowledge of English language would mean two things: *(i)* theoretical knowledge, and *(ii)* possession of the skills. Theoretical knowledge of a language could be by means of another language or it may be by means of the ability only to read and write. This will include all formal studies on the language such as grammar, its history, linguistics, and literature. The language skills consist in the actual possession of the language by means of *(i)* competence, and *(ii)* performance. The possession of the skills would mean, thus, the knowledge and exercise of the same.

(4) Language in its spoken as well as written forms is structured of two sets of elements: *(i)* structures and *(ii)* lexis. Structures in turn consists of *(i)* structural items and *(ii)* sentence patterns. Structural items (known as function words or grammar words) go into the ordering of the lexical items (also known as vocabulary items) in a sentence of the language. While structural words and sentence patterns are the concern of the grammarian, the lexis which from the bulk of a dictionary are the concern of the lexicographer who is specialised in the making of a dictionary. While articles, prepositions, conjunctions, auxiliaries, pronouns etc.

fall in the category of structural words, nouns, verbs, adjectives and adverbs which possess a definable conceptual content are grouped under lexical items (known also collectively as the lexicon of the language). Tenses, voices, reported speech, clauses, interrogative forms, forms of sentences etc. go under sentence patterns.

(5) Just as language is expression and content, it is also comprehension and content. While it is expression and content for the speaker, language is comprehension and content for the listener. These have significant teaching implications as will be discussed later.

(6) Spoken and written language consist of several sub-components: *(i)* sounds (letters), *(ii)* morphemes, *(iii)* words, *(iv)* phrases, *(v)* clauses, *(vi)* sentences, and *(vii)* discourses larger than the sentence. All these except sounds and letters possess the property of meaning of which further consist of sub-elements called, conceptual units.

(7) Language as expression consists of oral expression and written expression. These are also known as oral communication and written communication. Language as comprehension, by contrast, consists of listening comprehension and reading comprehension.

(8) Thus, language would, again be thought of as consisting of two major facets: *(i)* expression, and *(ii)* content. By expression we mean the extrinsic layer of language which consists of all forms from sounds to discourses as mentioned in (5); while the content of the language is the intrinsic layer known by the term 'meanings' studied under that area of linguistics known as semantics.

The structure of English language, as we have examined, is complex enough for an investigator to spend a life-time on it. The English teacher in the classroom, faced with the task of teaching English on the basis of a 'teaching unit' as the centre around which to move, will need to see language from several of the view-points examined above. English language as a set of sounds, and their combination in set patterns, the teacher is required to teach pronunciation; the spoken form of English language with all its phatic expression, patterns of stress and intonation, as well as forms of oral expression call for the teaching of spoken English. The English teacher has the major task of teaching the structures of English through structure (grammar) lessons. This will form the major bulk of teaching English at any level, especially in the case of L_2 learners of English in L_1 schools. Again, lexis consists of the major bulk of language both in speech and in writing. The lexical items occurring in a lesson in the textbook will be treated in vocabulary lessons. Reading and writing are 'considered the third and fourth skills of language. But reading can be for various purposes. Intensive reading lessons aim at helping the learners read some written material analytically and in detail taking into consideration all aspects of the language. Extensive reading lessons aim at the development of the fast reading skill and comprehension of the material in general. Again, there are compositions of various kinds aiming at helping the learner compose and give shape to discourses of various kinds. Oral composition lessons help the learner build discourses orally without any visual aid of a picture. In Picture composition lessons the pupils develop an oral discourse on the basis of picture which provides all the material in visual modality. The climax consists in written composition where on the basis of what has been discussed, the pupils write a discourse in the form of one or more paragraphs, a dialogue etc. Lastly, there is that aesthetic aspect of language, poetry, which the teacher of English at any level cannot forget. Appreciation lessons, thus, are meant to enable the pupils to get into the mood of looking at language as an art and a mosaic of sound patterns.

Apart from the fact that every lesson has a core in terms of the language content as we have seen, every lesson consists of a predominant skill as the fundamental aim of these lessons in English is the development of language skills. Every lesson is aimed at the development of one skill or other along with the pupils' acquaintence with the content matter of the lesson. Again, it must be emphasised that the teaching of separate kinds of lessons arising from a unit as well as the teaching of the skills are all ultimately aimed at the development and mastery of one and the same thing: English language, both in its written and spoken forms. It will be, therefore, the concern of the sections to place every lesson in English in relation to its language content on the one hand, and the skills on the other so that all this could be conceived as a unified experience amidst the great diversity of linguistic units.

3. Structures and Grammar Lessons

The structuralists were right when it was emphasised that language consists fundamentally of structures and that the teaching of a foreign language should consist of teaching the structures of the language *i.e.* in helping the learners actively use the structural elements of the foreign language. Teaching grammar which was confined to a few isolated classes in the grammar translation method has now become the centre of teaching English in schools. Structural items and sentence patterns are so fundamental that every English lesson is built around a particular item. A lesson in the textbook at the learner's disposal is a highly potential unit for the learning of the language. All things could begin from this Unit, as aspects of language learning evolving out of it. The lesson as a language teaching unit is representative or the embodiment of some structure.

Consequently, the structure embedded in a lesson is the very starting point of a series of highly interrelated lessons, as we are examining it throughout the present chapter. L_2 learning is considered chiefly the learning of the structures of the language. But under the present setup, and unlike in grammar-translation system, the structures of English are not committed to memory in terms of the rules of grammar, but the pupils are expected to internalise the structures by means of practice and constant acquaintances with the meaning and actual use of the structures of English. Therefore, instead of teaching 'grammar' as isolated lessons without any logical relation to the textbook, the teacher of English is expected to begin all the teaching of a unit from the teaching of the structure concerned, carry on the revision of the structures in the lessons which follow, and enable the learners ultimately to employ the structures in the construction of discourses which in turn will be useful for purposes of communication.

The structure lesson which will be the first lesson to follow from a teaching unit is, thus to be very well distinguished from the traditional 'grammar teaching'. The structures of English would include, as we have seen, *(i)* the structural items such as articles, prepositions, conjunctions, auxiliaries, comparatives, superlatives, question-tags etc.; and *(ii)* sentence patterns such as the tenses, passive voice, question forms, adverbs clauses, adjective clauses, reported speech etc. Teaching all other lessons including reading and writing is based on the work done of particular structures in class. The structure is therefore the central aspect of a teaching unit.

Speech Forms and Spoken English Lessons

Language is speech, and the teaching of English language would mean the teaching of the spoken English. It does not mean that English as a set of spoken forms exist separately from English as a set of written forms. The two sets of forms intercept in such a way that there are more elements common to both than there are differences because it is one and the same English language which is realised in speech and in writing. All the same, one may not deny that spoken English has a uniqueness which is characterised by several features of the language. For this matter, it is not possible to identify spoken English with written English apart from the fact that the two form separate skills of English language.

By a spoken English lesson we do not mean any listening-speaking lesson where the skills of listening and speaking will be predominant. By this we mean the teaching of elements which are peculiar to spoken English only and do not form part of written English. There are several features characteristic to spoken English that form the content of a spoken English lesson. The teaching of pronunciation forms the major bulk of spoken English lessons. Aspects of pronunciation, especially in English by contrast to the orthography of English, are so important that the learning of spoken English primarily means the learning of the pronunciation of English words, phrases, and sentences. For this reason, pronunciation lessons could be conceived as a unit separate from other aspects of spoken English. A pronunciation lesson would consist of a body of teaching techniques which are exclusively meant to help the learners acquire the correct pronunciation of the consonants, vowels, diphthongs, triphthongs, sound sequences (clusters) and words of English language. These are classes exclusively used (or purposes of teaching a particular set of items of pronunciation.

A spoken English lesson would consist of a body of teaching techniques to enable the learners of a particular level to acquire mastery over the use of items of spoken English such as the following: *(1)* patterns of intonation in English, *(2)* stress of English words which occur in day-to-day use as well as those that the learners are expected to pick up, *(3)* the proper use of weak forms in English, *(4)* forms of questioning, *(5)* the phatic expressions, such as the use of please, which occur in every day use, *(6)* ways of greeting people of various walks of life etc. A lesson in spoken English is structured so as to take care of anyone of these or other aspects of spoken English. Even though there are times when the teacher can take care of some of these during his regular teaching, such spoken English lessons will be of great value in countries like India where spoken English is the most difficult area of students to master.

Lexis and Vocabulary Lessons

If a spoken English lesson takes care of the specific features of spoken English, and a structure lesson teaches the structure used in the teaching unit, then a vocabulary lesson teaches the lexical items newly used in the unit. The textbook is constructed in a characteristic manner. Just as every lesson presents a new structure and revises one or more structures taught right before, every lesson as a teaching unit is constructed by means of some particular register of the language. A register consists of lexical items intimately related to one another centred on and generating from a particular life situation such as a profession, an occupation, a place, or an action of some significance in a community. A hospital would generate words such as doctor, nurse, medicine, patient, operation, injection etc. which are characteristically related to the life situation. The same would be true of professions such as those of a lawyer, a teacher, or an engineer or occupations such as those of a farmer, a carpenter, a goldsmith or a businessman. Every such life situation would yield a closely linked set of lexical items which can be worked out together into a discourse in the form of a descriptive paragraph, a story or a piece of conversation. What is significant here is that the teaching unit presented in the textbook for work in the classroom consists of such a register worked out into a set of descriptive paragraphs, a story or a piece of conversation.

At the same time, such a lesson in the textbook consists of lexical items which have already been introduced in preceding lessons, as well as there are quite a specified number of lexical items which are newly introduced. In doing so the textbook writer intends, on the one hand to acquaint the pupils with a set of new vocabulary items and on the other, help them revise the vocabulary items repeated in the lesson. The lesson is supposed to contain both active vocabulary for expression and recognition vocabulary meant only for comprehension purposes. The expression vocabulary should be so mastered as to be at the disposal of the child for active use in speech and writing; but the recognition vocabulary would be of help in listening and reading wbich involve an approximation of what the agent possesses with what is spoken or written. Just as the structures of English require separate treatment by means of a specific lesson tbe learners can be helped to work on the lexical items sufficiently enough to make it an active part of their language store.

Reading Material and Reading Lessons

Structures and vocabulary are the raw material which go into the making of a teaching-unit that we call a lesson in the textbook. The teacher after having completed work with the structures embedded in the unit and the vocabulary by means of which the unit is built up, has the next task to use the unit as reading lesson. A teaching unit prepared within the guidelines of the structural approach does not consist of an extract from any classical writing as the language, but the unit (lesson) is specially constructed around a situation employing the structures and vocabulary recommended for that unit. Attempts are made in such a unit to meet the following requirements: *(1)* a lesson is built up consisting of paragraphs or conversation so as to enable the pupils to use the same for purposes of comprehension; *(2)* the lesson is made suitable "to the level for which it is used by using only the kind of language as well as content material which will be within the grasping power of the particular level; *(3)* it is seen that the number of new words used is specific and that the most recent set of words taught is revised more, and *(4)* the content of the lesson *i.e.* the ideas expressed are neither beyond the grasping power nor below the 'take-in' level of the pupils.

The unit is used as a reading lesson with a specific view to developing the skill of reading material in English. By reading we mean silent reading only whatever be the proximate purpose of such silent reading. In the reading lesson we aim at two things: comprehension and the reading speed. These two factors are borne in mind while building up the passage for reading. Since the passage is to be read within a limited period only, a too lengthy passage would not serve the purpose. Again, if it consists of expressions and patterns which the pupils have not studied the passage would be considered the most inadequate because comprehension cannot be achieved of such a passage as well as every strange word or expression would be a hindrance for the pupils while reading. Just as speaking and listening consist of several sub-habits, reading silently requires the development of a number of mechanisms which we shall later be calling 'the mechanics of reading'. The lesson in the textbook furnishes the pupils with a systematically prepared material for purposes of developing the mechanics of reading with a view to achieving greater comprehension and faster reading in present-day circumstances when fast reading has become a great requirement.

Poetry and Appreciation Lessons

Teaching English poetry in L_1 schools has been a very controvertial subject. It has been traditionally held that the four basic skills of language are: listening, speaking, reading and writing. But this is only one view of language. Human language has dimensions greater than mere listening, speaking, reading and writing skills. The four skills have been defined as the functional off-shoots of linguistic competence. Human language has dimensions which cross the horizons of these functional off-shoots. Such dimensions of human language are its aesthetic, poetic, metaphysical and mystical applications. Even though these dimensions of language are rooted ultimately and concertedly in listening, speaking, reading and writing, language here crosses the horizons of its ordinary, communicational applications. Language is not an abstract system of symbols representing something with which it has no fundamental relationship, but human languages in trying to represent human experiences undergoes a process of unification with these experiences. For these reasons, language learning cannot be segregated from the linguistic dimensions such as poetry or literature.

All this would mean that there is an aspect very closely related to the four language skills, and this aspect is appreciation. Appreciation could be considered a language skill as authentic as the four basic skills, if we broaden the scope of the language skills. Appreciation can either be developed by means of listening to or reading the kind of language which is meant for the purpose. It is possible, therefore, to recite and appreciate, or read and appreciate poetry. Appreciation of poetry at higher levels of education such as the university could be called 'critical appreciation' when the individual person's critical judgement is called upon to enhance his sense of enjoyment. This is not the kind of appreciation that we wish our pupils to exercise. By means of various levels of poetry, beginning from mere nursery rhymes and going through full-fledged poetry, it is possible to develop in the learners of English a sense of appreciation for a language which is structured and organised for aesthetics effects. Teaching of poetry can be organised in such a way as to occur after the completion of one, two or three regular lessons in the textbook. If a particular textbook does not include poems of any kind, the teacher will have great pleasure in finding out and introducing good poems, in the class, and thereby providing the pupils with chances for appreciating the way 'sound harmony' is exploited in English language through poetry. Teaching English as L_2 can be complete only by the teaching of poetry which initiates the learners to the aesthetic applications of English language.

Discourse-building and Composition Lessons

The L_2 learners of English master a structure of English in terms of its meanings and uses of a set of lexical items by means of which the structure can be effectively used in a particular situation, and reads a passage which is structured of the grammatical items and the vocabulary. But the learning of English through a unit does not stop there. The learner is further led to make use of his knowledge of the structure and the vocabulary for constructing language units bigger than a sentence which we call discourses. Ability in constructing isolated sentences using the structure and the vocabulary is not the ends of language learning. The language is full of representations of life situations; the pupils are required to express themselves within the framework of situation. For these reasons, composition is considered to be the climax of learning English: when the pupils will be able to express themselves in related sentences on a given situation.

As the way language is expressed could be in a descriptive or narrative paragraph, or a piece of conversation, it is found better to call the same a discourse rather than a paragraph. The student of

English language can express himself in speech or in writing; in either the matter is composed in a specific manner. Consequently, we speak of oral composition and written composition. The aim is, again to develop the skills of oral and written expression. It is an attempt to get both the skills developed side-by side so that the one will have greater bearing on the other. In developing the skills of oral and written expression of a discourse, care is taken that both the discourses are thoroughly related. The aims are not to teach new aspects of language, but to help the learner organise what he has mastered upto a given time. For these reasons, it is recommended that the same discourse is used both for the oral expression and written expression. The pupils with the help of the teacher develops a discourse orally and then later expresses the same material in writing. But what is to be noted here is that oral expression and written expression are not isolated activities in the L_2 learning experience; they are so related to each other as well as to other language skill-based lessons that each is derived from a preceding lesson. If learning of spoken forms, and of a structure is the beginning, then composite oral and written expression will be the climax of learning experiences centred on a particular unit.

❒

7

Concept of Language, Teaching and Learning

Language is a means or verbal medium for expressing or communicating ideas, feelings, experiences and realisations. Language requires four basic skills—speaking, writing, reading and listening. Language is concerned with letters (alphabets), words and formation of sentences. The accuracy of language depends on the knowledge of grammar and correct pronunciation, correct spellings, correct reading and listening. Human beings have this privilege to evolve their languages for verbal interaction among themselves. Language is man-made communication device or means. There are several languages all over the world for communicating their feelings, ideas, experiences and realisations. Language is the means, not the end.

Language is used for the verbal interaction. Language is verbal as well as non-verbal. Non-verbal language is also known as body language or silent language. The realisations of a person are expressed through body language rather than verbal language. The verbal language is used for expressing ideas and experiences. The verbal language is well-developed scientific terminology which is used orally and also in written form. Non-verbal language is body actions or facial expressions.

Language consists of words which produce meaningful sound. Phonemes and morphemes are two important aspects of any verbal language. The words have their definite structure (morphemes) and create meaningful sound (phonemes) to communicate ideas and experiences.

The term language has been defined by several persons but some important definitions have been provided in the following paragraphs.

According to Ram Chandra Verma, "Pronouncing words and sentences for expressing ideas, feelings and experiences is called language."

According to Sweet, "Language reveals ideas and feelings through meaningful sound of words."

According to Plato, "Ideas and feelings are the realisations but when these are revealed through mouth is known as language."

According to Bholanath Tiwari, "Language involves the pronouncing organs which is used by a person according to his own for expressing his ideas and feelings to others."

Characteristics of Language

The following are the main characteristics of language:

(1) Language is the science of words and sentences.

(2) Language is the meaningful sound of words which is revealed through mouth organs.

(3) Language is the classical means of communication of ideas, feelings and experiences.

(4) Language is the most important means of verbal interaction among persons of a society.

(5) Language is acquired from the social environment of a person.

(6) Language is mainly acquired by social learning or by imitation. A child learns the language from his mother and that is why it is called mother tongue.

(7) Language is the skill of reading, writing, speaking and listening.

(8) Language deals with phonemes, morphemes, and grammar of words and sentences.

(9) Language is not the parental property, it is acquired and enriched through learning and practice.

(10) Language has not its final form. It is a developing and changing medium.

(11) Language is more traditional, it can be acquired but it can not be originated, but it is always a changing concept.

(12) Language proceeds from concrete to abstract ideas and imaginations.

Functions of a Language: The following are the main functions of a developed language like English language:

(1) A language develops four skills—speaking, writing, reading and listening.

(2) A language enables a person to communicate or express his ideas, feelings and experiences.

(3) A language is art as well as science which is acquired by imitation.

(4) A language helps for the verbal interaction among people to exchange their ideas.

(5) A language requires continuous practice and use for expressing thinking and imagination.

(6) A language helps for understanding phonemes (*pronunciation*), morphemes (*spellings*) and grammar for correct communication.

(7) A language helps in national development as well as national integration.

(8) A language needs mastery over it only to attain perfection.

(9) A literature is based on language which is the reflection of civilization.

A language implies correct pronunciation, correct spelling, correct usage of words, correct formation of sentences or use of grammar, but mastery of language refers correct expression for communicating ideas, feelings, experiences to others.

Importance of Language

Without a language a man is equivalent to an animal. Man is considered a super animal only due to his language, though it is evolved by man himself. It has its importance for a man as individual as well as social being.

(1) It is the most important means for acquiring human knowledge. The human knowledge has three phases—preservation, transmission and advancement which are possible only with the help of a language.

(2) A national language is the basis of national and emotional integration.

(3) It is the best and most applicable means of verbal interaction among people for exchanging their ideas and feelings.

(4) A language contributes directly and indirectly in the personality development of a person or child.

(5) The verbal interaction procedure is only the means of teaching in classroom.

(6) The history of a language is the history of human civilization.

(7) It is the best means for social and cultural development.

(8) The language is the basis of education. The national development is based on the education.

(9) The literature, culture, civilization and art development are written and preserved by the language.

(10) A language is the source of thinking and assimilation of ideas and imagination.

(11) The development of literature is based on its language.

CONCEPT OF TEACHING

The concept of *Task Analysis* is the main contribution of training psychology. Therefore, it is essential to understand the task of teaching if we intend to improve teaching. The task of teaching can be understood by the nature of teaching. Teaching is a social phenomenon whereas learning is a psychological phenomenon. It is difficult to define the term teaching as a series of acts based on the model of behaviour, which are appropriate to different kinds of situations such as form of government, form of society and social philosophy. Thus, the teaching behaviour has several dimensions. This teaching behaviour can be broadly classified under three categories—

1. Authoritarian teaching behaviour,
2. Democratic teaching behaviour, and
3. Laissez faire teaching behaviour.

1. **Authoritarian Concept of Teaching:** The type of teaching beahaviour is based on classical theory of organisation-task-centred. It has an assumption that members of organisation are primarily passive instrument, capable of performing work and accepting direction but not initiating actions. In this type of teaching behaviour, the teacher exercises a firm centralised control. He directs every action of his students. He does all the planning for the class and gives all the direction. He tells the students what to think as well as what to do. He thinks and regards himself as the only active agent in teaching and considers students passive listeners of instruction and information.

HC Morrison (1934) has defined 'teaching' according to authoritarian model of behaviour, "Teaching is an intimate contact between a more mature personality and a less mature which is designed to further the education of the letter."

In this definition Morrison considers that teacher is a more mature personality and student is a less mature personality. In the process of education, teacher helps in developing the students' personality by his intimate contact.

The teacher has the primary place and the student has the secondary place in the authoritarian teaching behaviour. The teacher is considered as an ideal model which student has to copy down.

2. **Democratic Concept of Teaching:** Teaching in the democratic form of government which is based on 'Human relations theory of organisation-relationship centred'. The main assumption of this theory is that members bring to their organisation attitudes, values and goals; that they have to be motivated to participate in the system of organisation behaviour. The attitudes and morale of the workers are important in the explanation of the organisation behaviour.

Edmund Amidon (1967) has defined the term 'teaching' in view of the democratic model of behaviour:

> "Teaching is deemed as an interactive process, primarily involving classroom talk which takes place between teacher and pupils and occurs during definable activities."

In this type of teaching, the teacher plays the role of democratic group leader. His main aim is to lead his students in the study of significant problems in the area in which he is teaching. There is always a scope in such a classroom for interchange of ideas, evidences, and insights, give and take, and respect for one another's ideas.

The teaching activities in this model recognised here are: motivating, planning, counselling and evaluation. Classroom talk can be classified and analysed.

3. **Laissez Faire Concept of Teaching:** Teaching behaviour in *laissez faire* form of government is based on 'Modern theory of organization: Task and relationship-centred'. It has an assumption that members of the organization are decision-makers and problem-solvers and that perception and processes are central to the explanation of behaviour of organization.

John Brubacher has defined the term teaching according to the laissez faire model of behaviour:

> "Teaching is an arrangement and manipulation of a situation in which there are gaps and obstructions which an individual will seek to overcome and from which he will learn in the course of doing so."

It is evident from the above definition of teaching that student is more active than the teacher. Teacher's job is to create the situation for the learner. The teacher leaves students 'on their own'. Here students but not the teachers decide what they want to do and how they will do it. This type of teaching may be organised even at reflective level.

Thus, teaching can be defined with reference to the form of government, but it is difficult to provide universal definition of teaching.

Another difficulty in defining the term teaching is that it has three dimensions: *(1)* Logic of teaching, *(2)* Technology of teaching, and *(3)* Semantics of teaching. The second type of teaching behaviour is characterised with a great deal of education in our country. According to our social conditions the following definition is most appropriate:

Educational technologist BO Smith has defined the term teaching universally.

"Teaching is a system of actions intends to induce learning through interpersonal relationships."

Teaching is that activity which influences learning but interpersonal relationship is an essential situation. The main focus of teaching is to enable the student to learn in all types of situations but the nature of interpersonal relationship may vary from situation to situation. It seems to be a comprehensive definition of teaching.

Modes of Teaching

A question of philosophy tends always to be framed in terms of concepts to be analysed and pattern of thinking to be clarified. The problems of philosophy are conceptual problems; therefore, when the philosophers of education wish to investigate the nature of teaching, they tend to ask not about teaching itself but about the concept of teaching, how it is used to do what sorts of things we do not. Their discourse tends to be focussed in a peculiar way upon the term 'teaching and learning' and their relationship to other terms.

A concept is the focus of inferences permitted by the various uses of a term:

> One way to study a concept is to explain how it is related to others, which concepts are connected with it and which ones are not.

"Teaching is the task of a teacher which is performed for the development of a child."

A close relationship exists between linguistic or conceptual analysis and the formulation of definitions. A concept is analysed by studying the meaning of its related terms, and a definition, like an analysis, is always a formulation of meaning."

The concept of teaching is immensely important to the philosophy of education, because it emphasises more fundamental:

"Teaching that... and teaching to... ."

Teaching someone that so and so... communication of knowledge and beliefs.

Teaching someone to do so and so... shaping behaviour.

Thus, teaching is for someone's development. The term development implies shaping behaviour and conduct; communication of knowledge and beliefs. The relationship between these two emphases in teaching is immensely important for the philosophy of education.

Instruction as a Mode of Teaching: The instruction is a kind of teaching which referes to teach someone that ... (communication of knowledge). It is more concerned with imparting knowledge and information. Training may be the pre-requisite for instructing. Instructing is good example of teaching. It acquires thinking, reasoning and generalization. It is a higher level of teaching.

Conditioning as Mode of Teaching: The conditioning is a kind of teaching which refers to teaching someone to do ... (shaping behaviour). It is more concerned with shaping behaviour and habits. It seems to be related with the concept of training and enters the teaching concept.

Training as a Mode of Teaching: Teaching is a kind of training. Training refers to teach some to do...(shaping conduct and skills). Training implies the manifestation of intelligence. Training is a poor example of teaching. Some persons have low intelligence, they are trainable but not educable. Teaching implies the higher degree of intelligence. Training is related to conditioning.

Indoctrination as a Mode of Teaching: The indoctrination is a kind of teaching which refers to the concept teaching someone that... (formation of beliefs). It mainly concerns with shaping beliefs. It requires higher order of intelligence, *i.e.*, reasoning with feelings. Indoctrination concerns with *doctrine* in way or transmission of doctrine. It is a good example of teaching.

Activities of Teaching

The teaching activities are those which a teacher performs in his classroom teaching. There are many ways to group the teacher activities or teaching tasks. BO Smith has classified teaching activities in cognitive and affective activities of teaching. Thomas F Green has classified teaching activities into three categories—

1. The logical activities of teaching
2. The strategic activities of teaching
3. The instructional activities of teaching

The Logical Acts: The logical acts are those activities relating primarily to the elements thinking or reasoning in the conduct of teaching.

Green has identified eight logical acts of teaching. These are as follows:

1. Explaining,
2. Concluding,
3. Inferring,
4. Giving reason,
5. Amassing evidence,
6. Demonstrating,
7. Defining and
8. Comparing.

The Strategic Acts: The strategic acts are those items that have to do primarily with the teacher's plan or strategy in teaching the material is organized or students are directed in the course of teaching. The performance of strategic acts of teaching is appraised by their consequences for learning outcome.

The analysis indicates that the different modes of teaching are distinguishable, but they are related to one another. These modes of teaching help in the development of a child. They all seem to be distributable along a continuum which represent the manifestation of intelligence. The continuum of teaching has been illustrated with the help of the following chart:

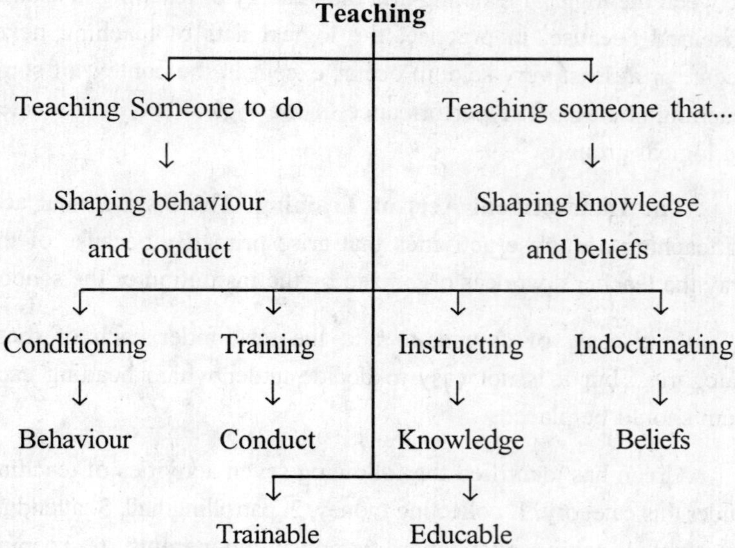

Modes of Teaching: "Teaching is an activity primarily concerned with manifestation of intelligence then it will follow that instructing is an activity which more perfectly displays the properties teaching than does indoctrinating."

Thomas F Green has identified the following seven strategic activities of teaching: 1. Motivating, 2. Counselling, 3. Evaluating, 4. Planning, 5. Encouraging, 6. Disciplining, and 7. Questioning.

Teaching can not occur independently without the logical and strategic acts. Activities associated with the logic and strategy of teaching are indispensable to the conduct of teaching wherever and whenever it is found.

The logical and strategic acts of teaching differ not only from the instructional acts but also from each other. They are distinguished primarily by the fact that performance of the strategic acts of teaching will be evaluated chiefly by their consequences, but performance of the logical acts of teaching will be evaluated independently of their consequences. This important difference between the logic of teaching and the strategy of teaching is usually obscured because, in practice, the logical acts of teaching never occur, or at least very seldom occur, except in the context of some teaching strategy. The performance of the logical acts is evaluated on logical grounds.

The Instructional Acts of Training: The instructional acts of teaching are those activities that arise primarily because of the way the teacher's work is organized by the institution or the school.

It is easy, of course, to add the test under each of these categories, but it is not easy to decide under which heading each item should be placed.

Green has identified the following seven activities of teaching under this category: 1. collecting money, 2. patrolling hall, 3. attending meeting, 4. taking attendance, 5. consulting parents, 6. keeping reports, and 7. chaperonage.

The activities of teaching can go without institutional activities of teaching. The institutional acts of teaching are distinguished because they are not necessary for the activities of teaching. The institutional acts of teaching, might better be known as the institutional activities of teachers.

The activity of teaching involves giving reasons, evidence, explanations and conclusions, it can be evaluated quite independently of its results in getting someone to learn.

The Objectives of Teaching

Teaching is a purposeful activity. It has the following objectives:

1. The purpose of teaching is to facilitate the learners, transformation of egocentric assimilation into true deduction.

2. The purpose of teaching is to help learner, adjust his perceptions to reality attaining harmony between internal organization and external experiences—*Piaget*.
3. The purpose of teaching is to help students to become better thinkers and doers.
4. The purpose of teaching is to help someone, some day, somehow, somewhere that he is able to see beyond and feel a new creativity to think and do.

Functions of Teaching

The teaching variables have important place in the process of teaching. The independent and dependent variables perform three major functions: 1. Diagnosis, 2. Prescription and 3. Evaluation.

1. ***Diagnostic Function:*** The teacher as an independent variable is more active in this function. He has to diagnose the entering behaviour of the learners and structure of the content for writing teacher objectives in behavioural terms. This function helps the teacher to take the decision about the following aspects of teaching;

(a) Entering behaviour of pupils

(b) Analysing teaching problems

(c) Individual variations,

(d) Content analysis in view of learning conditions.

The teacher uses two approaches in the diagnosis function. 1. A diagnosis test is administered for the entering behaviour of the pupils, 2. The content is analysed into elements and they are arranged logically in a sequence.

The student as a dependent variable diagnoses on the basis of this perception for his activities and responses. The language comprehensions, abilities, skills and expressions are the main comments of dependent variables.

2. ***Prescriptive Function:*** The teaching learning objectives can be achieved by the appropriate interpersonal relationship between the teacher and the student. The teacher takes decision about teaching strategies and tactics to be used;

The main objective of this function is to bring desirable change in learner's behaviour. Therefore, techniques of reinforcement are used for this purpose.

In selecting teaching techniques and feedback devices, teacher has to keep in mind the individual differences among the students. The teacher attempts to organize the intervening variables in such a way so that learning objectives may be achieved. It has two main elements:

(a) Teaching skills are taken into practice.

(b) The feedback devices are used appropriately.

3. ***Evaluation Function:*** The evaluation function is the most important aspect of teaching and its main objective is to examine the effectiveness of prescriptive functions. The criterion of evaluation is the realisation of objectives. If objectives could not be realised, it shows that prescriptive functions are not appropriate. Therefore, the weakness of the second function should be diagnosed, students should not be blamed for this weakness but prescriptive functions should be modified and improved. The evaluation function has two main activities:

1. Construction of criterion test, and
2. Evaluation of change of behaviour.

In the evaluation function the student is more active. He has to diagnose the items of criterion test and then he has to response. The student diagnoses the items on the basis of his achievements, abilities and skills. He attempts to check the correctness of his responses. The teaching functions are similar to a medical doctor. The main job of a doctor is to diagnose and to give a prescription. Thus, the source of teaching function is like medicine.

BO Smith has pointed out that knowledge and understanding of teaching function is basic information theory of teaching. Theory of teaching explain the relationship of variables and their structure.

Characteristics of Good Teaching

A good teaching is the main criterion of an effective teacher. An effective teacher has three types of characteristics: Presage, Process and Product factor. Teaching efficiency is considered the process factor. The characteristics of good teaching can be enumerated with reference to social structure and form of the government.

- Good teaching in a totalitarian state would be done by people whose personal interaction would influence learners toward valuing the goals of the state—which is good for the state is good for the individual.

- Good teaching in a democratic state would be done by people who arrange for a vigorous market place of freely announced ideas which force all learners constantly to adjust and assimilate their own values, structures, thought patterns, and total configuration of what they know.

The characteristics of good teaching of democratic model have been given in the following paragraph:

1. Good teaching requires appropriate responsiveness to the date, the child and group placing in the situation. The child activities can be rewarded properly.

2. Good teaching requires that the human environment should be accepted by each individual, that in some way it tells him that he is important. It suggests a personal report between teachers and students.

3. Good teaching requires a reduction in the controlling functions exercised continuously by the teacher. Teacher-behaviour should be indirect.

4. Good teaching requires that the teacher should be a well educated mature person who has the insight and energy for this demand job. It requires the responsive human environment that fosters exploration and initiative.
5. Good teaching requires that the classroom should be well managed so that the business of learning may receive full attention. Teachers perform the functions of controlling with clarity and with consistency.
6. Good teaching keeps or maintains the interpersonal relationship, supportive within the classroom. Out of this a shared problem-solving attitude develops.

Phases of Teaching: Philip W Jackson analyses the teaching systematically in three stages:

Stage I: Preactive Phase of Teaching

Stage II: Interactive Phase of Teaching

Stage III: Postactive Phase of Teaching

The each phase of teaching involves specific type of operations. These have been discussed here.

Stage I: Preactive phase of Teaching Operations

It is the stage of planning for teaching. All that a teacher plans before going to classroom to deal with students or to teach.

In preactive stage of teaching the following operations or substages are involved:

*1. **Formulation Goals:*** The teacher formulates in detail the instructional or teaching objectives in behavioural terms by using taxonomy of educational objectives. These objectives are of two types: Entering behaviour of learners and terminal behaviour of learners. These goals are based on psychology of the students as well as needs of the society.

2. ***Decision Making About the Strategies of Teaching:*** The teacher has to select appropriate strategies and tactics of teaching, keeping in view the nature and structure of the content and objectives of teaching. This operation is very important in teacher education programme. Such skills and abilities should be emphasised during the teacher-training courses.

3. ***Decision Making Regarding the Subject-matter:*** The teacher decides about the content to be taught to the students and the structure of the content (Memory, Understanding and Reflective Level). This decision is based on the following considerations:

(a) Demand of the curriculum prescribed for the students.

(b) The entering behaviour and needs of the students.

(c) Level of motivation of the learners.

(d) Teacher's preference for assessment relating to the content.

4. ***Ideas and Styles of Teaching:*** The teacher has to arrange subcontents in a logical sequence, in such a way that it should function empirically. It means that subcontents should be so arranged that it should facilitate the transfer of learning.

5. ***Development of Teaching Strategies:*** The teacher has to decide beforehand or in advance about strategies and tactics which he has to use during the course of his classroom teaching. When will he use questioning of lecturing, when will he show pictures, charts, models and when will he use blackboard, while recapitulation or evaluation, etc. These activities or sub-takes must be clearly decided by the teacher at pre-active stage of teaching for successful teaching.

Stage II: Operations at the Interactive Stage of Teaching

The interactive stage of teaching includes all those behaviours, activities which a teacher uses after entering the classroom. The interactive stage involves all activities in presenting the subject-matter.

According to P W Jackson (1966) the interactive phase: "The teacher provides pupils verbal stimulation of various kinds, makes explanations, asks questions, listens to students responses, and provides guidance."

The following are the activities at the interactive stage of teaching:

1. **Sizing Up the Class:** As the teacher enters the class, he perceives the size of the class and rolls his eyes upon the faces of the students. He locates or identifies spot which may be troublesome or helpful for him. He identifies which faces are discouraging, encouraging or apathetic to him. Thus, he tries to size up the class group before teaching. Similarly, the students also size up the personality of a teacher within a few initial seconds. The stage requires that teacher must look like a teacher first. His dress is most important.

2. **Diagnosis of the Learner:** The teacher tries to diagnose the levels of their achievements in his students in three areas:

(a) Abilities, *(b)* Attitude and interest, *(c)* Academic background.

P D A

Perception → Diagnose → Action

This may be done by asking some questions or enquiry.

3. **Action of Achievement:** *(a)* ***Selection of Stimuli:*** The stimuli in the action or activity of teaching can be verbal as well as non-verbal (verbal praise, gestures, expression through face, eyes), the way the teacher stands and moves around, etc.

A good teacher must know which one is appropriate stimuli or which is irrelevant stimuli in that particular teaching situation. A teacher should be able to select desirable or functional stimuli at once in view of the present situation before him.

(b) ***Presentation of the Stimuli:*** The teacher must know three things in presenting the stimuli: *(i)* Form, *(ii)* Context, and *(iii)* Order or Sequence.

(i) *Form.* In what form the stimuli should be presented so that proper motivation may be provided to the students.

(ii) *Order to Sequence.* The stimuli should be presented in a logical sequence so that behaviour repertoire may be established.

(iii) *Context.* The stimuli should be presented with some specific reference and context that it is irrelevant for objectives.

(c) ***Development of Strategies:*** The strategies of reinforcing the students, of controlling their verbal and non-verbal behaviour are used for imparting the subject-content effectively while a teacher teaches in the classroom.

Thus, the interactive stage involves three areas:

(i) Presentation of subject-matter.

(ii) Learning kinds (cognitive, affective, correlative).

(iii) Context of the learners (Background, Motivation, Needs, Attitudes, etc.)

The interactive stage generates the climate in the classroom which influences teaching-learning in classroom.

(d) ***Feedback or Reinforcement:*** It is a condition which will increase the probability that a particular response will be repeated in future. It may be of two types:

(i) *Positive Reinforces.* Which may increase the probability of reoccurring the desirable response or behaviour, *e.g.*, praise, appreciation, reward, knowledge of result, etc.

(ii) *Negative Reinforces.* Which may decrease the probability of reoccurring the undesirable response or behaviour, *e.g.*, reproof, punishment, etc.

The interactive phase of teaching refers to classroom interaction between teachers and students. The interaction may be classified into two categories: Verbal and Non-verbal. The verbal interaction involves two operations - initiation and response of teacher or student.

State III: Operations at the Post-Active Stage of Teaching

This is an evaluative phase of teaching. It includes the teacher task which evaluate student's performance based on classroom teaching. The behavioural change of students are assessed at the end of teaching. The oral or written questions are asked at the third stage of teaching. The following are the main operations at this stage of teaching:

1. ***Exact Dimensions of the Behavioural Change:*** The teacher evaluates the expected behavioural change with their actual behavioural change during his teaching. Most of the students emit the expected behaviour.

2. ***Selecting Appropriate Testing Devices:*** The teacher chooses certain suitable testing techniques and tools to measure the various desired dimensions of behaviour. The test should be reliable, valid and objective in nature. Cognitive and non-cognitive outcomes require different types of testing devices.

❒

8

Process of Reading, Writing and Spellings

One of the most valuable and useful aspects of learning a new language, is acquiring a mastery over reading the language. Learning to read with speed and comprehension is one of the most important skills that any educational system can impart, as it is through reading that one acquires the maximum amount of news, views, and knowledge.

Reading may be considered to be much more than a mere mechanical accomplishment. Reading for profit and pleasure, for these who have been guided to appreciate it, is one of the most important activities of life. It is one of the most enduring interests that a child can cultivate. A person who has not learned to read with pleasure, has missed out on one of the most enriching experiences on life. It is the duty of both parents and teachers to inculcate in the child a love for reading. Unfortunately, with the advent of the television, popularly and not incorrectly referred to as the "idiot-box" children have forgotten to read and think. Fed on inane, unimaginative and innocuous television programmes, a child in a modern Indian city is content to spend hours of inactivity glued to his set rather than be intellectually titillated by reading good, wholesome literature. In today's school set-up therefore, it is even more essential that good reading habits be instilled in children, which keep them reading not only to accumulate knowledge, but to spend their leisure hours fruitfully.

IMPORTANCE OF READING ENGLISH

Although reading for leisure adds a worthwhile dimension to every individual's personality, yet the fact remains that in India, few persons will acquire this interest to a great extent. For the majority of our pupils English will serve as a library language, and hence, reading or the ability to understand the written language, will be the most useful skill that they acquire in school. In this age, when there is a daily explosion of new knowledge, the skill of fluent reading plays a very important role in the life of every individual.

In school, the earliest attempts at reading English should be planned only after the children have had some training in reading in their mother-tongue. This removes the difficulty of trying to understand and read at the same time. Unfortunately this training is badly neglected in schools, and Indian students are rarely taught to read with ease and expression. Secondly, no new matter should be introduced in the initial lessons in reading. The earlier lessons in reading should contain only stories already known to the children. It is an error to assume that novelty increase the interest of the students. On the contrary, the fact that the child is able to read a foreign language correctly is an extremely satisfying experience, and provides psychological motivation for further attempts at reading. Only after the children have acquired a fairly large recognition of vocabulary through simple sentences and flash cards, should new material be introduced in reading lessons.

All reading lessons should be preceded by plenty of oral work. Only after a lesson has been thoroughly discussed and understood through oral work should the actual reading work begin. Meanings of new words should be discussed orally, and the child should become familiar with the sound and feel of the word, before he is called upon to read it. The importance of beginning every reading lesson with oral work has been emphasised by the structural approach of teaching English.

THE PROCESS OF READING

The process of reading may be broadly divided into three stages:

(1) **Recognition Stage:** At this stage, the learner is merely recognising the graphic form of the language, or the written symbols (alphabets) that constitute the written form of the language. His speed or slow progress at this stage will depend a great deal on the similarity of difference between the script of his mother-tongue and English. Generally Indian students find this stage difficult due to the great difference in script and pronunciation between English and the native languages.

(2) **Interpretation Stage:** This is the highest level in the process of reading, when the learner comprehends not only the meaning, but the significance of the language, *e.g.* the comprehension of idioms and other nuances and hidden meaning of the language. This stage is the ultimate goal of all reading activity.

(3) **Structural Stage:** At this stage, the learner learns to observe the syntactic relationships of the different items in the language and understands structural meanings. This stage helps him to accumulate grammatical rules that contribute to his acquiring mastery over the language.

These three stages seem to correspond with the three levels or language, *i.e.* phonological, syntactic and semantic. However, there is no rigid division of these three levels and each can overlap the other.

Mechanics of Reading

How do we read? How does the eye react during the reading activity? It is generally assumed that the eye moves in a smooth movement when it reads. The actual mechanics of reading show otherwise.

If you watch closely the eyes of a reader, you will notice that his eyes do not move slowly and steadily across the page in one even movement, but in a series of short little jerks. As soon as the concentration on the print is enough to see it clearly, the eye moves off, leaving it to the head to make the slow even motion, making the reader think that his eye is also moving slowly and monthly. The eye does not read while it moves. It recognises ordinary-sized print only when it stands still. It does not take much of a pause to make a recognition, about a tenth of a second is sufficient.

The small pauses of the eyes between jumps are called fixations, and the length of print or number of words covered between two fixations is called the eye span. A good reader has longer eye-spans and can take in longer stretches of the reading matter at once, while a poor reader has shorter spans, and consequently concentrates on small bits or individual letters.

The physiology of reading has exploded the old theory that one reads by spelling out words, and by seeing each letter in the word separately. One sees not one letter at a time, but entire words, and even phrases. The good reader sees words and phrases as a unit, hence the first reading lessons should deal with words instead of letters. For fluent reading, one needs along eye-span so as to see entire words and phrases at a glance. Close attention to letters not only discourages this, but builds up wrong habits which makes the development of fluent reading habits difficult. Most good readers pay, little attention to spelling and small typing errors. The eye does not analyse closely, but sees words as a whole. Only when the error is gross, and destroys the word picture is the mistake noticed. Good readers do not necessarily make good proofreaders for which close attention to detail and not meaning is necessary.

However, efficient reading includes not only the ability to see longer bits of language, but also the ability to comprehend the matter read. Since a reader with a longer eye-span can have a better Gestalt view of the matter, comprehension becomes easier for him. This implies the apparent paradox that a fast reader understands better than a slow reader. The reason is that for proper comprehension, an optimum speed is necessary. This aspect of reading can be compared to riding a bicycle, where balance is possible only after attaining a certain speed.

METHODS TO TEACH READING

Several methods have been used in India to teach reading English to children in schools. They have been of two types, the analytic and synthetic methods. The older methods were analytic in their approach, but with the growing influence of Gestalt psychology of teaching, synthetic methods are being used more frequently to teach reading to beginners. Some of the most popular methods of teaching reading are discussed.

1. **The Alphabetic Method:** This method was most widely in use since the early Greek and Roman days. It emphasised mastery of the alphabet, and familiarisation with the forms of letters. *e.g.* words were learnt by spelling out the alphabet such as c-a-t is cat. Letters were combined into words, and into phrases and a lot of repetition was required before mastery was attained. This was psychologically unsound, as the eye recognises words as a whole, and not individual letters. Moreover, English letters, often have two sounds *e.g.* c as in cat and cement. Often alphabets do not indicate the sound. Constant repetitions made this method slow and laborious. It is now used very rarely.

2. **The Phonic Method:** This method of teaching reading was adopted when it was realised that the sound and not the letters produce words. This method was followed in most Anglo-Indian schools and missionary schools for teaching reading to Indian students. Reading was taught with the help of sounds, which were broken up into consonant sounds and vowel sounds. This method is effective only when the sound of letters corresponds with the pronunciation. This is not an adequate method for teaching English words, as often the sound of letters does not indicate the pronunciation, *e.g.,* c as in cake and cement (difference in sound of c). Many times, words may have the same sound, but meanings

and spellings are different *e.g.* rite, right, write. Moreover, many English words have a silent consonant, *e.g.*, palm, might, knife etc. The phonic method proved to be inadequate for teaching reading of English in India as pronunciation of words often differ from their spellings, and in focussing attention on word recognition, this method failed to develop comprehension of the matter read.

3. **The Word Method:** The word is regarded traditionally as a minimum meaningful unit. The word method makes use of words presented in meaningful settings, and is learned mainly by the "Look and Say" method. This procedure is based on the assumption that each word has a characteristic form of its own. For establishing meaningful associations, pictures often accompany the words in readers. Attention of the pupils is also directed to the details of words such as syllables and their sounds.

The main strength of this method lies in the fact that equal attention is given to word meanings and word recognition. Its greatest drawback however, is that the necessary accuracy and speed of reading required of a good reader become difficult to achieve, and hence this method is not very popular with teachers of English these days. Many times, the word is lengthened into a phrase for the purposes of teaching, but the phrase too has the same limitations as the word, with the result that the Phrase Method of teaching reading is not a very effective method either for teaching reading.

4. **The Sentence Method:** The sentence method is based on sound psychological principles of a sentence being a complete unit of thought, speech and writing. Therefore, a sentence is the most natural unit for teaching unit.

The initial activity in the class involves the attention of the pupils being directed to some topic of interest in the class. As the children begin to discuss this, they make many interesting statements one or two of these statements are put by the teacher on the black board, and read with expression. Children are then directed to discover groups of words in the sentence, and specific words within each group. Later lessons repeat words introduced earlier, so that children become familiar with the words.

The sentence method has been found to be the most effective method for teaching reading to beginners. It is in keeping with the Genstalt view of learning, which pays greater attention to the whole sentence and discourages word-by-word reading. It stresses the meaning of what is read leading to an intelligent reading attitude. In his book, *"The Psychology and Teaching of Reading"*, Schonell states, "One of the greatest values of the Sentence Method lies in the help it offers to the pupil from the context and from the continuity of meaning that can be embodied in the material."

The sentence method lays the right foundation for a thoughtful reading attitude, due attention paid to word recognition and comprehension and for developing a keen interest in readings.

5. **The Story Method:** This is an expansion of the sentence method and is based on the belief that stories have a universal appeal for children, and hence an interest in reading can well be developed through this method. The story is also a more complete and interesting unit of thought than a sentence, as it carries the reader through an entire series of events. It is more advisable to use this method at a later stage of teaching, after the children have acquired a fair amount of recognition vocabulary. Thus, it can well be treated as a sequel to the sentence method of teaching reading to slightly older children.

The story is first presented to the class orally, so that new words are introduced in their proper context, and the disadvantage of trying to understand what is being read is removed. Attention of the pupils is drawn to the difficult words and phrases as written in the text book. As the sequence of events is already known children soon begin to identify and recognise sentences in the story. Only familiar and already discussed stories should be taught for reading lessons to beginners, as the belief that novelty adds interest to the activity has been disproved by modern researches. The very fact that the child is successfully able to read a few sentences of a foreign language provides a great sense of achievement, and is a strong psychological motivation for creating interest in reading. The best approach to teaching reading to beginners would be a combination of the synthetic methods of word, sentence and story with due attention being paid to both meaning and word recognition right from the beginning.

TEACHING OF WRITING

Writing is of immense importance. Developing the skill of writing as an important factor in teaching of a foreign language is listening, speaking, reading and writing. Writing skill reinforces oral and reading work. The language items already learnt become firmly fixed in the minds of students. Writing provides a change of activity helping in reducing monotony and enables the students to do some homework.

Writing helps the organisation of thought by enabling a person to have before him at the same time the different points which he is trying to present. Without the help of writing, it is very difficult to keep in the mind the various aspects of a subject.

Referring to the importance of writing, Bacon says, "Reading makes a full man, conference a ready man, and writing an exact man."

Mahathma Gandhi has also emphasised the importance of writing by saying, "Fair and legible handwriting makes a man perfect in all walks of life."

In the words of Bell, "Writing is a tool used to enable us to express, what is in our mind and for some people is almost as important as speech."

Bell has given a statement about teaching of writing as follows: "Writing is a difficult art; it required complete control of the muscles of the hand and wrist and this control a small child does not naturally possess."

So there is a need to teach writing English. It involves the following aspects:

(1) Teaching to develop the skill of controlling the small muscles of the fingers and the wrist, while writing.

(2) Getting students do various exercises in written work.

(3) Teaching coordination of hand and eye.

In the early stage stress is given on handwriting only. At later stage the ability to write in English is needed in college and university where one has to take notes from lectures delivered in English as well as from the books and journals published in English. Students should be enabled to write English correctly and legibly. After completing education in colleges, the ability to write in English is needed in offices too because English continues to be the language of administration at the central level.

Characteristics of Good Handwriting

Following are the qualities of good handwriting:

1. ***Legibility:*** Handwriting should be legible and easy to read. Illegible handwriting creates a very bad impression on the reader. Bell says: "Illegible handwriting in a young man or woman is a sign of untidy and careless mind."

2. ***Simplicity:*** Letters, should be simple, bold and free from all extravagant strokes and flourishes.

3. ***Distinctiveness:*** Each letter should have a characteristic form of its own.

4. ***Uniformity:*** There should be regularity in the size of letters. The proportion between their heights and width should be correct and uniform.

5. ***Speed:*** Children should be able to write neatly and legibily at normal speed.

6. ***Spacing:*** The letters in a word, the words in a line, and the lines in a page should not be crowded too closely together.

7. ***Adjustment between Writing and Thinking:*** It implies that there should be no omission of words or phrases due to quick thinking in fast writing.

8. ***Beauty:*** Handwriting should be pleasing to the eye. A beautiful handwriting is one in which the letters are well-formed, even in size, and suitably spaced, which is upright or slopes slightly forward, and in which the lines of writing are parallel to the top of the sheet of paper.

Writing is a difficult art which needs practice and great attention. Therefore, FG French has suggested that training in writing (Penmanship) should begin with training in muscular control through fairly large movement using fingers in tray of sand or chalk, or brown paper. The movement should include drawing of lines of various lengths and direction, half circles, strokes, etc. The child's hand should be fully in various movements.

Preparation for Training of Writing: Before teaching writing there is a need for proper preparation. This step has three aspects as follows:

(a) The first is free hand drawing. The writing work should begin as an exercise in art. The students should think they are having practice in art work. The teacher should allow them to draw on the chalkboard or large sheets of brown paper fairly large shapes of various size and direction.

(b) The second is controlled drawing, *i.e.* the above shapes should be drawn within lines on the paper to give controlled practice to children.

(c) The third is acquaintance with written forms. Students should become well acquainted with written forms before practice in writing begins. For this, the teacher may write the names of the pupils on their books, desks or other belongings. He may also write labels on boxes containing different materials.

In this way students become interested in writing.

Teaching of writing provides initial training in learning to write and starts with script writing. It is convenient to know about writing scripts.

Writing Script: English letters have their origin in Roman script. At present, English has mainly three kinds of scripts:

(1) **Printed Script:** Print script is the type of writing which pupils come across in their textbooks. The letters in this script are not joined together and is thus easier to learn. The common practice is to start with script and turn to cursive writing after a year or two.

Advantages of Printed Script: The advantages claimed for beginning with script writing are:

1. Since little children have no control over their hands, it is easier for children.
2. It follows the maxim of, 'from easy to difficult'.
3. It has beauty, cleanliness and clarity.
4. Beginners also find it easy.
5. No strokes are needed to join the letters. As such letters in print script have simpler form than in cursive script.
6. There is lesser need for supervision of the pupils than in teaching cursive script.
7. Children can compare their letters with printed ones. Thus they can find their errors in the formation of letters easily.

8. Less eye and physical strain is involved in the learning of print script than is involved in learning cursive script.

9. Print script is suited to the muscular and motor development of young children.

Disadvantages of Printed Script: The following are its limitations. Printed script has certain disadvantages too. They are:

(1) Some letters, *e.g.*, 'a', 'g' sometimes appear alike in print script.

(2) It cannot facilitate speed which is essential for good handwriting.

(3) It consumes much time and energy.

(2) **Cursive Writing:** Cursive writing is the running type of writing in which the letters in a word are joined together with strokes or loops. In this type of writing, pupils can learn to write at the maximum possible speed. Most of the English knowing people all over the world make use of it. It is always better to help the students to write in the cursive style. If once they form the habit of writing in print script, they will find it somewhat difficult to switch over to cursive writing. Pre-primary school children, however, find it difficult to learn this style and it is better to teach them writing in the print script in the beginning.

However, in spite of its drawbacks, modern methods of teaching favour print script. Research findings also are in favour of beginning with print script. It was found that better scores were obtained by those pupils who first used script writing and then changed over to cursive writing at an early stage than those pupils who always used cursive writing.

(3) **Rounded Cursive Script:** It is also known as Marion Richardson's script. In it, only some letters of a word are joined together. Since it combines some characteristics of both print and

cursive scripts, it has the advantage and disadvantages of both the kinds of scripts. Keeping in view, the advantages and disadvantages of print script and cursive script, it is advisable that during the first two years, print script should be taught, as *The Handbook of Suggestions for Teachers* says. "In the beginning, the symbols used should resemble those they (pupils) have been accustomed to see in print." After that, cursive script must be 'introduced. A pamphlet of *British Board of Education* says, "The end is to equip the individual with a final cursive handwriting, which is facile and legible."

General Considerations to be kept in Mind While Teaching Writing: The following general considerations should be kept in mind while teaching writing to the beginners:

(1) *Choice of Script:* The choice of script is the first important consideration to be kept in mind while teaching writing to the beginners. The teacher must decide which script—print or cursive—should be introduced. The script writing consists of plain letter forms usually based on straight lines and curves; where as the cursive writing consists of running letter forms joined together by links and loops.

We write, almost all of us, cursive hand. The running hand although, has unnecessary curves to join the individual letters. The writing tools, *viz.*, pen, pencil and chalk is not to be removed now and the as is done in print script. This writing in cursive script saves time. This ensures greater flow and facility. But this is only possible with old learners to maintain such flow of letters and words from his pen. But for a class who begins English early, it is advisable to begin with the print script. It involves easy strokes for its being simple and clear.

(2) *The Choice of Style:* Another consideration to be kept in mind while teaching writing to the beginners is the choice of style. The teacher must decide which style is more

convenient. It is easy to imagine that the child can draw scratches more conveniently than circles.

There are mainly two styles of writing: *(1) Vertical* and *(2) Slanted*. In vertical style letters are written in vertical fashion (/) It is the best style of writing. The slanted style is of two types: *(a)* Forward slant (/), *(b)* Backward slant (/).

(3) Writing Material: Writing material also needs careful selection in the beginning. The material is to be provided which makes for the desired movement of the muscles involved in writing.

To achieve the movements of arms to be regulated, provide broader/rough surface in the children to start their initial writings. The initial writing consists of free lines, stokes, curves, circles and dots, etc. The children can start writing with soft chalk. The purpose is that they should acquire easy movements and develop hand and eye co-ordination. At the later stages they should learn to write on paper. For this, large-sized soft lead pencils should be used. Pencil-writing should be followed by writing in ink.

(4) Posture: Posture is an important consideration to be kept in mind while teaching writing to the beginners. Children should be made to adopt a good posture while they are engaged in writing. When at their desks, they should sit comfortably in their seats in a correct position. Their both feet should rest on the ground. The body should lean slightly forward from the hips, but should not touch the desk. The head should be so held so that his eyes are about 13 inches away from the paper. The chest should be clear of the edge of the desk. Both forearms should be within two or three inches of the elbows and should rest lightly on the desk.

METHODS OF TEACHING WRITING

There are four methods of teaching writing or penmanship:

(1) ***Kindergarten Method:*** It is based on the principles of Kindergarten method of education. Under this method, a Kindergarten box is used. In it, there are pieces of wood or plastic of different shapes. By joining these pieces, the letters of English alphabet (both capital and small) can be formed. Pupils are given practice of constructing letters of the alphabet by joining those pieces. Following are the merits of the method:

(a) It is based on play method.

(b) It is interesting.

(c) It is easy.

(d) It suits the nature of little children.

But this method has the following demerits:

(i) In India, teaching of English generally starts from class VI. Students of class VI belong to (10-13) age group. So, it is not appropriate to use kindergarten box at this stage.

(ii) Pupils might have learnt writing their mother-tongue through this method they may not, now, take interest in this method.

(2) ***Tracing Method:*** This method requires the learner to make movements over the printed or written letters with a pen or pencil held in his hand. The letters of English alphabet are either written in dotted lines or in a frame with lining. The teacher writes letters in this manner in the notebooks of the students and asks them to pass their hands over the letters. Exercise books for this are also available. There are certain merits of this method as follows:

(1) Children learn by imitation and this method follows the principle of learning by imitation.

(3) Montessori has also recommended this method and asked students to pass their figures over sand paper letters.

(3) There are no chances of wrong learning.

This method has the following demerits:

1. It entirely depends upon learning by imitation and in this way, it hinders the development of the ability of free writing.

2. It does not handle properly individual differences. All students reach up to the same level of development.

3. It discourages the habit of hand work.

(3) ***Free Imitation Method:*** Under this method, pupils copy in their notebooks the model letters written by teacher on the blackboard or notebooks or written in books. Bell suggests that the model letters should be written on flash-cards. Since students imitate or copy the model letters with the help of their own imagination and retention power, it is called free imitation method. This method has the following merits:

1. Pupils get a chance to show their ability and skill.

2. Individual difficulties can be traced and removed easily.

3. They become self-dependent.

Following are the demerits of this method:

1. In copying, there are chances of mistakes.

2. Due to mistakes, there is slowness in development.

3. The teacher has to work hard in pointing the mistakes of copying.

4. If the child copies some words incorrectly, he learns it for ever.

Stages of Teaching Writing

The teaching of writing English should go through the following four stages:

The first stage is related to motivation. First of all the pupils should be motivated to learn writing. The teacher, for this, can use various motivational techniques.

The second stage is very important. It is related to penmanship, *i.e.*, giving knowledge of writing letters of the alphabet.

After some practice in drawing ,the child starts learning to write the letters of the alphabet. He learns small letters first and capital letters afterwards. To start with, the child does not learn the letters in their order but by groups which contain letters of similar shape. For example:

1. Letters made by strokes, i k l t w x y z can be presented in one group;
2. Letters formed on the circle, *viz.*, c e o in another group;
3. Letters formed by circles and strokes, *i.e.*, a b d p q in third group.
4. Letters formed by curves, *i.e.*, f g m n r u in the fourth group.

The teacher should demonstrate the shape and form of the letters on the chalkboard. The students will carefully observe the teacher's demonstration and then imitate and practice writing the letters on four-lined copy books.

Learning the Alphabetical Order: Towards the end of the first year, the order of the letters in the alphabet can be taught in the following manner:

(1) Capital letters group one is round letters based on circle, *viz.*, OCQ.

(2) Capital letters group two is letters formed by strokes, *viz*, A I L E F M N V W X Z.

(3) Capital letters group three is based on curves; *viz.*, B D J P R S U Y.

There is no rigid rule for selecting a particular group for teaching writing alphabets. The teachers can form their, own groups in the light of these suggestions.

The third stage In this writing words and sentences should be taught. Side by side, emphasis should be given to beautiful and uniform writing. For this, exercises should be done as follows:

(1) Caligraphy: A model word or sentence is written on the first line of the exercise book. Students are asked to write the same word or sentence many times below the model word or sentence.

(2) Coping: Pupils are asked to copy word, phrases and sentences from the black-board or book. The teacher takes a round of the class and supervises the written work of students. According to *Bhandari, Hinkley* and *Ram*, this exercise has three main *advantages*:

(a) It reinforces the new structure.

(b) It helps the pupils to learn the conventions of writing capital letters and punctuation.

(c) It fixes the correct spelling of words.

(3) Dictation: In Indian schools, dictation has two objectives: *(1)* to educate and *(2)* to examine. The main aim of dictation can be stated in the words of *Wein* "The aim of a dictation lesson is to produce in the class a one hundred per-cent accurate passage of writing, also to install into

their minds the idea that correct spelling and punctuation really matter and than nothing less than absolute accuracy is good enough—in fact to produce a spelling conscience."

Steps of Dictation: While doing dictation, the teacher should go through these steps:

1. Selection of the paragraph;
2. Supervising the writing aids;
3. Getting students prepared to take dictation;
4. Telling spellings of the difficult words of the paragraph;
5. Dictating the paragraph;
6. Model reading of the paragraph;
7. Re-reading of the paragraph;
8. Correlation: *(i)* by the teacher *(ii)* by the student himself and *(iii)* mutual correction; and
9. Practice of the corrected words.

Advantages of Dictation: It has the following merits:

1. It helps co-ordination between hand and eye, hand and ear.
2. It facilitates listening and understanding.
3. Errors of writing can be checked.
4. It initiates self-activity.
5. It gives practice in taking notes.
6. It improves the understanding of punctuation.
7. It increases the ability to be attentive.
8. It follows the principle of learning by doing.

In the fourth stage In this the pupils learn mastering a mature style of handwriting.

Students are initiated to composition writing without any help. The following graded exercises should be done, as suggested by *C. S. Bhandari* and his *associates*:

1. Construction of single sentences and writing them.

   Examples. She is my mother.

   Dinesh is a naughty boy.

   Go there.

2. Construction of sentences in sequence and writing them.

   Examples. Rajesh is my friend.

   She is a beautiful lady.

   Tomorrow he is going to Delhi.

   There he will meet his brother.

3. Building up short paragraphs and writing them.

   (a) Students describe a picture in a paragraph and write that.

   (b) They re-write a given paragraph.

   (c) They construct and write a paragraph on the basis of keywords.

   (d) They construct and write a dialogue.

4. Writing more than one paragraph.

5. Writing letters.

6. Writing free composition, *i.e.*, writing compositions without any restriction.

7. Writing stories.

TEACHING OF SPELLINGS

To write correct words is solely dependent upon the knowledge of spelling. There is also competitive value of spellings. In competitions, the students express themselves through language. For this, writing correctly is very essential. Besides, to appreciate the English literature, students must possess thorough knowledge of spellings. Due to all those reasons, it becomes necessary for an English teacher to know about the teaching of spelling. It is universally admitted that English spelling is full of difficulties. The reason is that it is anomalous and inconsistent. Moreover, it does not correspond to the pronunciation. For example, *see, sea; die, dye; grieve, deceive,* are differently spelt although their pronounciation is very much the same. The unreasonable and unsystematic nature of English spelling makes the Indian pupil confront very serious difficulties, but he can do nothing except to confirm to the established spelling.

Characteristics of English Spellings

The spelling of English is, in the words of Emest Weekly, 'quite crazy'. Logically, there should be one symbol or letter for one sound, but in English there are only 26 symbols or letters for 45 sounds. As a result, there is quite a lot of confusion about English spelling. The Editor of *The Times of India* has very aptly put it, 'The student is embarrassed to find that there is one r in 'harassed' and is harassed to find that there are two rr in 'embarrassed'.

The English teacher should know the pecularities of English spelling. It will facilitate his work of teaching English spelling. Some worth mentioning pecularities are as follows:

1. ***Homophones:*** There are words which have some sound but are spelt differently, *e.g.,* cellar, seller.
2. ***Silent Letters:*** Many letters are not pronounced, *e.g.*, *r* when it comes before a consonant.

3. ***One Letter Different Sounds:*** Each letter of English alphabet stands for two or more sounds.

Teaching of Spellings: This question has been engaging the attention of the teachers of English for a very long time, should spellings be taught?

Their conclusion as supported by recent experimental investigations is that spelling should not be taught. WS Tomkinson says, "Spelling is caught rather than taught" The teaching of spelling should therefore, be incidental. Spelling drill is simply wasteful and ineffective.

There are no hard and fast rules for spelling. Hence, the only thing that can be done to teach correct spelling is to develop in pupils the habit of reading carefully. Wither Spoon writes: "The only way to learn to spell correctly is to read carefully, to notice the correct spelling of words, to study the proper order and arrangement of the letters, that form the words, and to impress the correct image of the words in the mind."

For Indian students, it is essential to teach English spelling, because, in India, English is a foreign language. The following are the methods of teaching spelling:

(1) Old Drill Method: This method is also known as traditional method. Rote Memory Method is its still another name. Under this method, a list of words is prepared according to their importance. The teacher asks the students to cram the spelling of these words one by one. This method is advantageous because:

(a) Students learn the pronunciation of words too.

(b) Students can know the spelling of many words during a time.

(c) Since there are no certain rules of English spelling cramming is best.

(d) It is based on the principles of faculty psychology. But this method has following disadvantages:

(i) The list prepared by teacher contains some such words which are not used in daily life.

(ii) Generally teachers prepare the list of words without giving any attention to a standard.

(iii) This method is dull and mechanical.

(iv) Students cannot understand how and where to use the crammed words.

(2) Incidental Method: Under this method the teacher tells the spellings of only those words which come across while reading the way the textbook. It means the way the spellings are taught is incidental. The one advantage of this method is that it correlates spelling with reading.

(3) New Drill Method: The New Drill Method is the same as the *old drill method*. The only difference is that in it the list of words is not prepared arbitrarily. The words are chosen on two bases:

(i) Needs of pupils, and

(ii) Use of words in text-books.

In this way, this method overcomes one disadvantage of old drill method. But it has all the other disadvantages which Old Drill Method has. Its advantages are also the same as Old Drill Method has.

(5) Dictation Method: Although the sole aim of dictation is not spelling teaching, yet it can prove useful therein. *Bhatia* and *Bhatia* observe, "Dictation is not so valuable as a device of teaching as of testing spelling. It fixes the spelling of words more firmly in the mind." To make dictation more workable in spelling teaching the teacher should write the difficult words on the black-board and then rub them.

*(5) **Play-Way Method:*** The play-way method of education can be applied to teaching spelling. Some spelling games are as follows:

(i) One word is written on the blackboard. Students are asked to form words out of the different letters of the word, *e.g.*

Copy: Cat, ocean, picture, you.

(ii) Different words can be formed from one word, *e.g.*

Child: children, childish, child-like.

(iii) One word is written on the black-board. Students are asked to form a word beginning with the last letter of the word. Then, students are asked to form a word beginning with the last letter of this word and so on, *e.g.*

Book-know-wolf-fat....

(iv) Spelling competitions can be held. For instance:

The class is divided into two groups. One group says one word. The other group has to find words beginning with the last letter of the word given by the first group and so on.

(v) The teacher writes some words on the blackboard and asks students to watch them carefully. Then, he rubs the blackboard and orders the students to write those words in their notebooks.

(vi) The teacher writes the spellings of some words leaving some letters of each word. Then, he asks students to fill in the gaps. For instance:

ma...ket, f...th...r, ta...le, cha...r :

The method is based on activity. Students find it very interesting. It does not put unwanted load on pupils memory. This method is found more advantageous at junior level.

(6) Transcription Method: Transcription means copying from black-boards, flash-cards or books. Under this method, students are asked to transcript words from black-boards, flash-cards and books. In this way, spelling can be learnt because:

(i) It forms mental pictures of word, and

(ii) It fixes the material firmly in mind.

(7) Dictionary Method: The students should be asked to consult dictionary to know the spellings of words. This method helps them in later life. This is also a self-learning method.

CAUSES OF WRONG SPELLING

We can find many students making spelling mistakes inspite of the efforts of the teacher. Some of the causes of poor spellings are:

1. **Irregularity of English Spellings:** The most important cause of poor spelling is the irregularity of English spelling. In English, we find many such words which have correspondence in spelling and pronunciation, but difference in spelling, *e.g. to, too, two.. right, write, wright,* etc. In the same way, there are many words which are similar in spelling, but different in pronunciation, *e.g., cut, put, come, home; bound, wound*. This irregularity is still greater in words which have one or more silent letters: *e.g., knee, hour, night, might,* etc.

2. **Unsuitable Methods of Teaching Spellings:** The methods which teachers generally use for teaching spelling are unsuitable. Moreover, the methods are incomplete, uninteresting and haphazard. The method which the teachers generally use is the Drill Method. They ask the pupils to spell words aloud collectively and in a singing manner. This method is mechanical. It ignores the needs and difficulties of individual child. "It is incomplete and onesided." It does not take into consideration the different memory types: i.e., oral, visual, motor, and auditory. Some teachers ask the pupils to learn lists of words.

3. **New Methods of Teaching:** New methods of teaching like *sentence method, word method,* and *look and say method*, have taken the place of old methods of teaching such as spelling method and alphabetic method. In the new methods, the attention of pupils is drawn not to the letters that form the words, but to the general shape or pattern of a word or a sentence.

4. **Indifference of Teachers:** Most of the teachers are indifferent to pupil's spellings. Their main aim is to finish the course in time and make the pupils cram up important things for the examination. They do not lay a stress on dictation, transcription, and written composition which go a long way to improve spelling.

5. **Over-emphasis on Oral Work:** In the words of Bhatia and Bhatia *"The over-emphasis on oral work in the initial stages of learning English is regarded as an important cause of poor spelling. It naturally depreciates the importance of written work and it is in writing most that we need to know the correct spelling."*

SUGGESTIONS TO IMPROVE SPELLINGS

The following suggestions can help teachers in improving the spelling of students:

1. While teaching spelling of words, they should be grouped on the basis of meaning of spelling or pronunciation.
2. Different methods of teaching spelling should be employed.
3. Spellings should be graded.
4. The teacher should pay attention to each student individually.
5. The teacher should make a list of words which most of the students mis-spell.
6. Students should be encouraged to keep pocket dictionaries.
7. They should be asked to keep note-books and note down spellings of difficult words.

8. Use of different types of audio-visual aids can help a lot.

9. Extensive reading can help in improving spelling.

10. JM Rice concluded after conducting a series of researches that fifteen minutes a day be given to spelling.

11. Students should be encouraged to use spelling exercise books.

If the teacher keeps in mind the above suggestions, he can surely improve the handwriting of students because, in the words of H. R. Bhatia. "To spell one's word correctly is a part of the courtesy due to the person who is to read what is written and the absence of it is considered a lack of good education and respectability."

❐

9

Audio-Visual Aids

The teaching objectives are achieved in terms of behavioural changes among students. "The teacher generates the learning situations so that desired behavioural change may be brought about. The behavioural change of students is the means to achieve objectives of teaching. Therefore, teaching is organised in view to achieve teaching objectives and learning structure. The teacher selects the appropriate teaching strategies and tactics to create the desired learning structure and conditions. Organising teaching is the second step of managing teaching learning. It includes the following activities:

(A) Selection of Appropriate Teaching Tactics

The teaching process is not a simple one but it is a very complex process. The teacher uses several strategies and tactics. The teaching tactics are selected by the teacher to generate learning situations on the basis of teaching objectives and nature of the elements of the content. Educational technology has given the concept of 'learning experiences' so far but the researches are being conducted for developing criteria of selecting appropriate teaching tactics.

The teaching tactics are ways of applying a teaching strategy for achieving the learning objectives. The definition of teaching tactics has already been given in the chapter of 'Teaching Strategies'. One teaching tactics is used in various strategies of teaching. The teaching tactics are meant for generating appropriate learning structure.

Learning structure concept is originally given by Robert Gagne as, conditions of learning but Davies has used the term 'learning structure'. The meaning and definition of learning structure have already been presented in the chapter of 'Relationship of Teaching and Learning'. The following five learning structures are more useful for a teacher to select appropriate teaching tactics:

1. Signal structure of learning.
2. Chain structure of learning.
3. Multiple-discrimination structure of learning.
4. Concept learning of structure, and
5. Principal learning of structure.

(B) Selection of Appropriate Communicaton Media

Media and method are used interchangeably in education, but they are quite different to one another. These can be differentiated in the following manner:

(1) The universe has two major components: *(a)* space and *(b)* time. If we assume instruction as a universe, this way has two components: *(i)* instructional space, and *(ii)* instructional time.

The '*institutional space*' is covered by radio and television. A teacher can reach interior parts of the country and can knock at the door of students. The *media* is essential for instructional space.

The '*instructional time*' is governed by lecture, question-answer experiment, story-telling and dramatisation, etc. A teacher imparts the knowledge and information to his students by employing a method at a particular time. The instructional time is known as method.

(2) Another way to distinguish between media and method is that method is an abstract entity which is determined by

the nature of the content. For example, information through lecture, facts through story-telling or dramatisation method, concepts through experiment are taught to the student.

The media is a concrete entity which is determined by the mode of communication. The mode of message communication is known as media. For example, information through radio, facts through television are communicated to the students. The media of communication are: radio, television, video-tape and tape-recorder, etc., and mode of communication through various media are speaking-listening, writing-reading and visualising-observing.

The media and method are not contradictory to one another but they are complementary and supplementary to one another. A method can be made effective by using an appropriate media of communication.

Theory of Communication: The basic communication model involves an informational or interpretative process in which messages, information or reaction to information travel from the initiator to receiver through the route called communication channel. The message conveyed by the teacher or the educational media may be verbal or visual and the receiver may listen or see and react in other ways. The communication channel in the classroom should ideally carry both messages and counter-messages; it involves initiation, reception and response which serve as feedback. The communication must keep open, as only when the teacher and pupils are able to communicate clearly and without interference of understanding and ensure appreciation. But unfortunately many interferences and communication barriers arise which impede the smooth flow of communication between the teacher and his pupils in the classroom, *e.g.*, advertisements and entertainment's media. The communication channel employs media of teaching and learning. Type of communication channels have been described here.

Types of Communication Channel: There are three types of communication channels:

1. ***Speaking-Listening:*** In this type of communication, an interaction is face-to-face as in the case of a teacher. There are situations when the listener can share feelings of the source in the same way as in the case of eye-to-eye contact. Listening to the radio is an example for this type of communication channel.

2. ***Visualising-Observing:*** The observer is physically separated from its producer and yet is able to feel the impact of the ideas conveyed as in motion film or television. The dramatisation is an example for this type of communication.

3. ***Writing-Reading:*** In this type of communication channel, the 'decoder' is physically separated from the 'encoder' all the time and yet the decoder is able to enjoy and appreciate the feelings of the author. Reading for an instruction material is an example for this type of communication channel.

Through these communication channels a sender or teacher conveys his message through some media to a receiver or *vice versa*. The function of a sender is to encode the message and receiver student has to decode it.

(C) Selection of Appropriate Audio-Visual Aids

The communication strategy, teaching strategies and tactics are selected for achieving objectives and generating structure. The audio-visual teaching aids also play a significant role for this purpose. The learning structure can be effectively generated with the help of audio-visual aids and teaching objectives can be achieved easily. Therefore, the audio-visual aids are termed as educational technology one, *i.e.*, hardware approach to teaching. It is an old view that audio-visual can be used to make lesson interesting and involving more than one sense in teaching learning situation. The students can be made active and attentive by the use of teaching aids. The research studies have yielded that a particular audio or visual aid may be used to achieve a specific objective of learning or specific learning condition may be created.

Characteristics of Audio-Visual Aids

The following are the five important features of audio-visual aids:

1. It helps in developing perception of learner.
2. It facilitates in understanding and comprehension.
3. It aids in positive transfer of learning and training.
4. It increases the retention of the learner.
5. It provides reinforcement to the learner.

These are the generalised statements about the audio-visual aids, but teacher has to take decision in selecting appropriate audio-visual aids on the basis of students-level and objectives of learning. The most crucial feature of teaching aids is to help in creating appropriate learning structure.

Types of Audio-Visual Aids

Initially the origin of teaching aids is from physical sciences and engineering. This use of audio-visual aids has mechanised the education and teaching learning process. BF Skinner comments that our kitchens are more mechanised than education. This statement seems to be true even in our country. The audio-visual aids are classified into three categories:

1. Audio Teaching Aids: This type of teaching aids facilitate audio senses and encourage the listening function. The audio sense is more active by the use of such teaching aids. The audio sense is active in lecture and question-answer strategies. The use of tape-recorder, radio, record player and gramophone make the learner more active and attentive in teaching process.

The students take more interest when lesson is displayed with the help of such teaching aids. These aids produce only sounds.

The audio aids are used to realise the cognitive and affective objectives and can not be used in achieving psychomotor objectives.

*2. **Audio-Visual Teaching Aids:*** These teaching aids are used to facilitate both audio, and visual senses and encourage listening and observing functions. Thus, these aids involve more than one sense simultaneously and the learner is more active. This is most effective and useful than earlier aids. The learning structure can be generated more easily and comprehensively. These aids develop the perception of the learner which is the basis for the understanding of any concept. Television, films, and video tape are the examples of audio-visual aid. These are costly and rarely used in teaching learning situation.

*3. **Visual Teaching Aids:*** These teaching aids facilitate the visual sense and encourages the seeing function. The visual sense is more active by the use of such aids. This sense is more active when teacher uses pictures, maps, graphs, models and line drawing in his teaching activities. No teaching can be possible without the use of such teaching aids. The visual teaching aids play a significant role in teaching: geography, physics, chemistry, biology and economics, etc. The geography content cannot be taught without the use of maps and globe. Generally visual aids are most useful and economical than audio-aids. Generally visual aids are used most frequently in all teaching situations. The audio teaching aids are costly and rarely used but most useful in language teaching. The language laboratory has been designed for this purpose.

The visual teaching aids are used to achieve the cognitive objectives but affective and psychomotor objectives can also be achieved.

Selection of Appropriate Audio-Visual Aids

The audio-visual aids have a significant place in organising process, but selection of appropriate audio-visual aids is challenging task for a teacher. There are various types of teaching aids, hence selection is the complex problem. The various criteria and principles are used as the basis for selecting appropriate teaching audio-visual aids. The studies conducted in this area have revealed that learnitig objectives and learning structure seem to be important criteria. The effective audio-visual aids may be selected by employing both criteria:

1. Teaching-learning objectives, and
2. Learning conditions or structures.

The practical outlines on the basis of research findings have been summarised here.

1. Learning Objectives as Criterion for Audio-Visual Aids

The most important criterion in selecting the appropriate audio-visual aids is the learning objectives. The objectives formulated in planning phase should be considered as criterion for taking decision about the teaching aids. The following are the research conclusions in this regard:

The cognitive and affective objectives may be achieved by the use of radio, still pictures, films and educational visits. The cognitive, affective and psychomotor objectives are realised with the help of tape-recorder, record-players, television and language-laboratories.

The line-drawing is used to achieve the cognitive objectives.

The models are effectively used to realise the affective and psychomotor objectives.

2. Learning Structure as Criterion for Audio-Visual Aids

For an effective use of audio-visual teaching aids, it is essential that learning structure should also be taken in consideration, because learning objectives can only be achieved by creating appropriate conditions or situations or situations of learning. This, appropriate teaching aid facilitates appropriate learning structure. Several Studies have been designed and conducted in this direction. The effectiveness of this teaching aid has been evaluated in terms of learning.

Multi-Media Approach

It is evident from the term multi-media that more than two media of communication are involved in a learning package or instructional procedure. A teaching content of a subject varies in nature, therefore, it can be best presented by employing various media of communication. Moreover, it facilitates the individual variation of the learner. Now multi-media packages of learning are developed.

This multi-media approach has been tried in our country, in NCERT and at the Centre of Educational Technology (CET) as the mass media for in service teacher-educators. This experiment has involved the multi-media packages which has the following components: Television programme for 22 minutes, radio programme for 20 mts. Pre and post television for 1 hour.

The multi-media approach is useful for the following area of education:

(a) Distant education for study,

(b) Non-formal education programme,

(c) Correspondence education, and

(d) Adult education programme.

'Satellite Instructional Television Experiment (SITE)

It is recent development and innovation in the media communication. It is the most effective media of communication in the field of education. Television broadcast has the limited range but by using satellite its range has been extended. The International Telecommunication Satellite Consortium helps the member-nations in broadening the area of operation of the television communication by means of orbit satellite. The satellite are/is launched at a height of 22,300 miles up over the equator in orbits. This satellite serves as television relay station.

The SITE is the outcome of the long-standing debate started in the country by space scientists and educational technologists who have proposed a national satellite for television and communication. An Application Technology Satellite has been made available in India by the National Aeronautical and Space Administration of the USA for a period of one year from August 1975. The SITE of India was inaugurated by the Prime Minister of India on 1st August 1975.

The one-year long SITE which was completed on 31st July 1976. The SITE programmed reached the rural population of about 3-5 million spread over 2400 far flung villages and in six Indian states: Andhra Pradesh, Bihar, Karnataka, Madhya Pradesh, Orissa and Rajasthan. The SITE programme was telecasted in the morning and evening every day. The SITE stations were located at Sambhalpur in Orissa, Gulbarga in Karnataka. Hyderabad in Andhra Pradesh, Jaipur in Rajasthan, Muzaffarpur in Bihar and Raipur in Madhya Pradesh. The SITE relay had reached nearly 5,000 villages in these states in 1980.

The Objectives of SITE Programme

The SITE is an unique programme with varied purposes. The general objectives of SITE are as follows:

1. To ascertain the workability of satellite-based instructional television system in our rural areas.
2. To show the potential value of SITE in the rapid development of effective mass communication.
3. To stimulate national development in our country with important economic, technological and social development.
4. To demonstrate the potential value of satellite broadcast television programme in the practical instruction to the children and adults of rural villages.

Uses of Satellite Broadcast Television Programme

After considering SITE project, the following recommendations have been given for the use of SITE:

1. It can be used to disseminate information about specific aspects of science, agriculture, technology, health and family planning.
2. It can be used for both in-school and out-of-school education.
3. It must be used in the developmental process as an instrument of social change and national cohesion.
4. It can be used to develop a scientific attitude and to deal with the day-to-day problems.
5. It can be used effectively for adult-education, non-formal education, distant education, correspondence education and extension programmes of agriculture.

The SITE can be used in the following areas:

1. In service Teacher Training Course.
2. In technology-learning situation, *i.e.*, instructional and educational programme.
3. Programme on agriculture.
4. Adult-education and Non-formal education mainly distant education.
5. Health and family planning.

Educational Programme Through SITE

The educational programmes of SITE have been designed to suit the needs of children of primary and pre-primary age groups. The following are the main objectives of educational programme:

1. To improve their basic concepts and skills in the areas of language, numbers and social behaviour.
2. To develop a positive attitude for formal education among children by making the process of education interesting, creative and purposive.
3. To make them aware of the process of modernisation of the life and society around them and change their attitude in this direction.
4. To promote aesthetic sense and habit of health living.

The SITE programmes for children are so designed as to acquaint them with facts and matters normally beyond their usual observation. There should be three main focus on such programme:

- To develop instructional skills.
- To develop right type of attitude towards education.
- To develop desirable habits among children.

The SITE programme can also be devised for Teacher Education Programme to understand the importance and use of this programme in their teaching learning situation.

Closed Circuit Television (CCTV)

It is the recent development and innovation of media communication in the field of education. The signal is sent to the receiver using co-axil cable in CCTV programme and the range dependents on the length of the cable. The CCTV can be used effectively in educational institutions. It has the following advantages:

1. It enables educational institutions to present televised instruction according to their own needs and requirements.
2. It magnifies exhibits and demonstrations which are normally difficult to observe in a classroom teaching situation.

3. It increases the range of instruction far or more location beyond the classroom.
4. It gives the opportunities for exchanging teachers and courses between one institution and another linked to a circuit.
5. In teacher-teaching institutions CCTV with video tape recorder can be used for proving the feedback to the public-teachers. "Micro-teaching can be effectively used by using CCTV with video tape.
6. CCTV is being used in medical colleges when an operation is being performed. It can bring the world of reality to the home and to the classroom.

Limitations: It has the following limitations:

(1) There is no personal contact with the teacher.

(2) It is a one-way communication.

(3) It is very costly and complicated, an average teacher can not use it.

(4) It encourages the passive form of learning than active seeking.

Importance of Satellite Television

The experiments of Satellite Instruction Television have shown that it improves the quality and effectiveness of instruction or as media of communi-cation. Thus, it has the relevance for developing countries:

1. The SITE is estimated to have cost over Rs 100 million. The system for India is also true like other developing countries.
2. The SITE has the greater significance in domestic use in the developing countries.

3. The SITE can carry sodo-economic development for the villages and it is possible to follow-up the greater awareness and educational knowledge created in the villages.
4. The value of SITE is beyond the monetary investment or even the immediate results.
5. India is ready to design and execute a nation-wide television system and uses this medium to educate the masses in rural areas and it is also possible to extend this facility to the whole country.

In short, experiments and research studies of SITE have shown that educational television seems to be effective for instructional purposes. Therefore, it must be an inseparable segment of over-all classroom environment.

MODERN AID TO TEACHING ENGLISH

"Good instruction is the foundation of any educational programme. Audio-visual teaching aids are a component part of that foundation." In these words, Francis W Noel reflects the opinion of many modern educationists, who are attributing a growing importance to audio-visual aids for making any teaching-learning experience more effective. The term "audio-visual aids" includes all means, techniques and the various paraphernalia which a teacher uses to catch the eyes and ears of the pupils, to distinguish them from the conventional methods of teaching which use only language. The senses are the very foundations of and knowledge for it is through sense-impressions that we obtain knowledge of the outside world. We also learn to adapt ourselves to the environment through our senses.

Until recently, all formal teaching was carried out through the medium of language, but in recent years educators have come to lay more emphasis on learning through the senses, particularly through the sense of sight; as research findings on this subject have shown that the great majority of students learn more readily through sight than through any other sense. Hence materials used for teaching that employ both the senses of sight and sound are popularly known as audio-visual aids.

Most materials that can be used to help make teaching more vivid and impressionable are visual aids such as pictures, charts, models, maps, etc. But in teaching language, aids that make use of the right sounds are more important, as language is primarily a system of communication by means of sounds. For the teaching of English, it is very necessary to have teachers who have a good command over the language and who speak the language well. There is however, a great paucity of such specialised teachers, and therefore, in the present-day context, modern aids to language teaching acquire a greater significance. Audio-visual aids have great possibilities in the teaching of English, but it should never be forgotten that they are primarily aids to a teacher and that they can never replace a good teacher, who teaches with her effective voice, her sparkling eyes, her facial expressions and her gestures, and whose presence is more important than any teaching aid. Audio-visual aids, no matter how modern and impressive they may be, are mere tools in the hands of a teacher who should know when and how to use them.

SOME MODERN LANGUAGE AIDS

(1) **Radio:** The radio can present a comprehensive course in language teaching, and can be an integral part of language teaching programme in even the most backward places where electricity is not yet available, thanks to the easy availability of battery-operated radios, which are not really expensive. Hence, even schools in the far flung rural areas and distant villages can integrate radio lessons into their daily time-table. One of the greatest advantages of a radio as an aid to teaching English is that it does not involve any heavy expenditure for either purchase or maintenance. Secondly, a radio lesson is not affected by the size of the class, which is usually a

fairly large one in a poor and developing country like India. A radio lesson also fosters the listening habit in children, which is an important stage of learning a new language. As far as the actual spoken language is concerned, the radio can present the true form of pronunciation, intonation and stress on which all good language teaching must be based. A further advantage is that the radio can employ the services of the best speakers or the language and of expert teachers of English, whose impact can be felt by a very large section of the student population. Vivid narration of interesting stories, dramatisation of short plays and expressive recitations of well-loved poems can all contribute to make language learning a living and pleasurable experience through the radio. One of the biggest drawbacks of radio lessons is that they lack visual stimulus, and can become boring if not handled imaginatively. Moreover, there is only one-way communication, for the students cannot participate in the discussion. Nor is there any opportunity to modify teaching according the individual needs of some pupils.

(2) **Tape Recorders and Record-Players:** Both these modern aids to language teaching are very useful, as they help in teaching and instilling right pronunciation habits in children. Listening to recordings on tapes or records can form an extension activity of teaching English. One of the most important uses of the record-player is the use of "Linguaphone" records prepared by the British Council, based on books like "Better Spoken English", which give useful exercises in simple English and have short and interesting poems making use of different vowel and consonant sounds and consonant clusters. There are also exercises based on intonation, stress and rhythm of continuous speech. A teacher of English can profitably exploit these excellent records for acquainting the pupils with a real "feel" of the true spoken language.

One of the greatest advantages of the tape-recorder in the teaching of English is the opportunity it provides for taping the pupil's own, voice. Many times, children do not realise the mistakes they make in, pronunciation and intonation, but when they hear their own voices taped and played back, they can get a clearer perception of how and why they make errors.

(3) **Language Laboratory:** One of the modern concepts in language teaching is the belief that a laboratory for teaching languages is as important in any educational programme as a laboratory in different science subjects. A language laboratory is a separate room with several booths having taping facilities and hearing facilities with head phones, which are controlled by a central monitor from which the teacher can direct the activities of all the booths. The main advantage of such a laboratory is that a teacher can attend to several children at the same time either with pre-recorded exercises, or with spontaneous utterances devised to suit every individual pupil's need. A teacher speaks first as a model, and the pupil repeats, which is then played back to him. Or the teacher can ask questions and the pupils answers.

(4) **Films:** Films have a powerful influence on the pupils as they appeal not only to the eyes and ears but also to the emotions, which can lay a firm foundation for right attitudes and habits. Films have a universal appeal with children, and this appeal can be usefully exploited by a teacher of English to supplement reading material. Well produced films on such well-known novels in English literature such as Jane Eyre, Oliver Twist, The Mill on the Floss, Gone with the wind or dramas of Shakespeare and Bernard Show can acquaint the pupils with the life, manners and historical significance of the times. The atmosphere of different ages too can be portrayed through such films. Many excellent films prepared by BBC can be obtained easily by educational institutions and shown in the school as a regular feature. The tremendous impact of films on children's minds can be seen by the great interest that the film "Gandhi" has recently provoked both in India and in other countries.

Modern electronic devices like the video tape-recorder (VCR) has made it possible to bring well produced films of BBC and educational films from America, Canada and Australia to the classroom very easily, This is however, a very expensive device too, and is not widely used in schools in a poor country like India.

TEACHING LANGUAGE BY TELEVISION

(1) **TV as Language Teaching Medium:** The language teacher is limited by the four walls of the classroom and can bring in the outside world only in a limited way by means of make-believe and mime. Television can help in widening the language experience of the pupils. The greatest merit of television as a language teaching aid is that it can create a far greater variety of situations than the teacher. Children can be exposed to the language at a railway station, at a bus stop, in various home situations etc. Television provides an opportunity to a large number of pupils to learn from a single experienced teacher. A good television teacher provides a model of correct speech not only to the pupils but also to the less gifted classroom teacher. Unobstrusively, television programmes for the pupils help to train the classroom teacher.

(2) **Limitations of Television:** Television of course is not without its limitations. It is a uni-directional medium—a one way communication. Thus, it can never replace the classroom teacher who has the advantage of being in direct communication with her class. Television can do only some things better than the classroom teacher. Broadly speaking, language teaching consists of presentation, practice and production. Television can handle the first stage *i.e.* presentation very well quite often better than the classroom teacher because it has access to a wide variety of audio-visual aids. But television is not as well suited for the second stage *i.e.* practice drill, due to the lack of feed-back from the pupils. However, there should be some practice drill in the TV programmes as it involves the pupils directly. Besides pupil participation, practice drill also serves as a model for the classroom teacher. The third stage *i.e.* production is the least suitable on television because the medium is unidirectional.

(3) **Attitude:** The attitude of the classroom teacher towards television programmes is very important. At the initial stages the

teacher has to be convinced that the television teacher is not a threat to his existence. The television teacher is not going to replace him but is working with him. What is even worse is the attitude of the teacher that the TV period is a bonus free period for him. The right attitude can be developed through teachers, seminars, where the teacher is also trained in the use of the medium by demonstrating the work in all period. In any TV period the classroom teacher plays a larger role than the television teacher.

(4) **Types of Programmes:** Television lessons can be syllabus-based or enrichment programmes. Purely enrichment programmes would be a luxury we would not indulge in with our limited resources. Nor would they be desirable at the very early stages of language learning because the cultural background of the language, or programmes on literature would be irrelevant to the pupils at this stage. Our teachers bound as they are by examination would not accept purely enrichment programmes. An essential pre-requisite to enrichments programmes is a very broad based educational system. Thus our programmes would have to be based mainly on the syllabus with an element of enrichment.

(5) **Team Work:** The television teacher uses additional unusual resources related to the course *i.e.* aid to learning which are not normally within the classroom teacher's reach and he also provides expert teaching to a vast number of pupils at the same time. But he cannot do this without the classroom teacher serving as a link with pupils. The classroom teacher does this by preparing the pupils for the TV lesson helping the pupils during the TV lesson and doing the follow-up work to carry on where the television teacher left off. Thus a TV period consists of:

(i) Pretelecast Activity (by classroom teacher).

(ii) Follow-up (by classroom teacher).

(iii) TV Lesson (by television teacher with the help of classroom teacher).

The classroom teacher and the television teacher must communicate with each other.

(i) Teachers notes in which the television teacher informs the classroom teacher what to do for the telecast and follow-up work and how to help during the TV lesson, *e.g.,* when to make children repeat after the TV teacher and when to listen.

(ii) The television teacher must also visit schools regularly in order to exchange views with the classroom teacher directly, help her if necessary and view that lesson with the pupils.

(iii) Evaluation check sheet which the classroom teacher must fill in after every lesson to report to the TV teacher the impact of the TV lesson in the classroom.

❐

10

Principles Governing the Choice of Textual Selections

What specific materials for an English course should be chosen? It is an outstanding question before the designer and the administrator of all courses of English studies. The tripartite segments in the task of learning are being managed by the learners, by the organisation of learning (teacher and methodology) and the source material. The last one of the three should help: *(i)* in acquiring language skills, *(ii)* in using language after acquiring it in fruitful and effective way, and finally *(iii)* in generating ideas, thoughts, appreciation, mood, attitude, and sentiments that help in expanding the horizons of cognitive-affective domain of the human mind. The treasures of materials are exceptionally important to receive our attention at large, if generations of mankind are to be liberated from the crippling influence of practice or drills of numerous varieties.

Over the past few decades, we have exercised our minds in pinpointing the various methodological trials in the teaching of English; next, the 'objectives' of learning. English assumed the importance when they came to be analysed into major and minor components; and now, the learner-centred approach is engaging the attention of the present day class teaching. In the labyrinth of different hints and processes, we seem to have lost the sight of a learner, at whatever stage he was, gleaming with a curious joy when he suddenly experienced a few sparkling ideas or, caught some uncommon but flashy imagination, or encountered some difficult stages of comprehension while reading something abstract or having to grapple with a word in an entirely new situation. No matter, what his standing in the class was he was seen delighted to catch hold of story books of different make and of diverse themes. He would not leave the book till he finished it, his homework might have remained untouched till the next visit to the school. He appeared completely lost in his own world; the magic touch of handling a book brought for him tons of joy than do our practices and drills in communicative teaching in our classroom these days.

Certain viewpoints pertaining to the selection of materials for English courses of study may give rise to controversy. Still, some points of view are worthy of consideration. In the selection of material for an English course we find ourselves faced by two significant questions. What specific material, literary or otherwise, is to be chosen? And how can this selected material be placed to the greatest advantage? Since both the problems are exceedingly complex and cannot be easily or, completely solved, we shall never come to regard our individual courses as being finally and satisfactorily fixed—either as to choice or arrangement of material. Yet, out of all the complexities certain principles emerge to act as helpful guides.

Some decades ago, some schools used to inherit their courses in English or, else legally borrow them (till the thirties and forties of the present century). They were books published abroad but selected for our schools and for different grades. Subsequently, some practical difficulty arose because of relatively larger number of pupils continued to crowd the classrooms and thus the organisers, not being able to cope up with a number of problems, in an independent country, felt that the existing textbooks did not meet the needs of the day. Rigorous training for teachers for teaching English for few suitably selected candidates of English only continued for a decade or so. Large number of candidates of mediocre ability got enrolled for teachers' training. Teaching English always occupied a very important position in the teacher training curriculum. Experts from abroad viewed the teaching of English from an entirely new angle. Selections from English literary works were thought unnecessary; English language, in its structural analysis brought in some hope in the sense that the build up of sentence construction gained all importance, whereas, literary ideas in the study materials behind the sentence construction received a back seat. English, it was felt, if it was to be taught, must be taught in basic structural fashions and that too following a direct method. The situational-notional idea did not yet gain ground. The learners would learn English by imitating the teacher speaking in English in the class. The 'speech' in the class was highly controlled by simple to difficult structures; naturalness in speech had to be abandoned; artificiality in language practice prevailed by and large; books were written in the simplest fashion bereft of any 'idea building' or imagination growing. At present, the most prevalent opinion for retention of English courses in our schools has taken sides with common, popular, easy-to-use English writings. The main course book should develop students skills for reading for understanding, writing, listening and speaking. The course book should extend their vocabulary. For such cheqeured outline of objectives, some themes are sampled out somehow. The themes are claimed to centre around high interest-level of learners. These interests are enumerated around People, Adventure, Environment, Mystery, Children and Sports and Games. Now around these 'interest' zones, quite a few lessons have been carved out to provide for class lessons. The core idea behind the selection of lessons around the themes is to develop students skills in reading, writing, listening, and speaking. Language if it is to be learnt, must be spoken, must be used for communication and interaction at large. Hence, the learning of language must be efficiently testified in its 'use' in day-to-day living.

A few observations need to be considered. Should our boundary of objectives of learning English be limited to only the development of LRSW? Could not the boundary be extended to expansion of ideas, to enjoyment of reasoning, to explanations beyond stereotype, and to appreciation of beauty and style, to even creation of new forms of expression of unique novelty? Children of the present era appear to be quite ready for varied and enriched exposure to abstract thinking and enriched experience. The course book, thus, need not limit its scope to mere vocabulary expansion but can engulf much more—both in cognitive and emotive realm. Secondly, how were the 'interest zones' limited to the seven or eight opinionated ones? Could not they be more, or different 'interest zones'? At least the bases behind selecting these high-interest areas are not clear. Perhaps the fancy for populist compositions in English on themes around incidents and activities of daily life, on local adventures, simplistic performance in games and sports, on scientific operations, on communications of all types, have caught us on the wrong side to favour the inclusion of such write-ups in the selection of many of our text books. We cannot miss the sight of the 'inner soul' in the human organism who is attempting to learn a new language. He cannot feel satisfied with the structural elements of hundreds of hundred type that make the outward form called the 'language'. He has to look up to the 'agent', the teacher who puts 'life' into language, who brings forth the initial touches through meaning that is infused into the collective composition of Structures. Someone should generate in the learner a keen desire to articulate the new combination of sounds, a desire to understand the simple, open, clear meaning as expressed in the theme, to relish and remember the 'piece' long after the theme has been taught and even get reawakened sometime later, may be in an absolutely new surrounding. Language learning bereft of sound meaning and joy in the company of ever-new ideas, is meaningless, even if it is a second language or a third. Therefore, we cannot prescribe any course material without keeping an eye to the learners' enjoyment and thereafter, the interest grows and not before.

Take for instance, music. In music, the excellence in singing brings forth the typical style and musical nuances in the elaboration of the lyrical contents when a singer presents the renderings in a characteristic way. The music reflects the individuality besides interpreting the poetic contents in a highly evocative mood. The singer makes use of a lyrical composition in a subtle haunting rendering, using the beat or the time-cycle suitably set to the choicest rhythm. But the external dressing alone and independent practice of different elements/notes would not bring forth the desired result. The music must have the best of mood of the singer, as a result of which the superb renderings can pour out to project the poetic sentiments. Thus music is created. And then a master mentor's typical mannerisms may be seen reflected but the disciple interprets the poetic content with his/her individuality.

Coming back to our resource material. We wish to broaden our investigation, to discover in the lawful principles of selection an answer that will have wider application and prove of more universal guidance:

1. We need to encourage a common ground of academic approach. A common interest among the schools may have important academic value, that may reveal other nature and civilisation. Those framing an English course should usually select for their classes the books that are generally read. That will encourage a certain kinship between different cultures. To this end a small group of literary selections should be chosen for reading practically in every high and higher secondary school. In the past, from the middle grades upward through the secondary classes, abridged/unabridged editions of noted English writings, such as, "*The Tales from Shakespeare*" (Charles Lamb), "*A Tale of Two Cities*", or, "*David Copperfield*" (Charles Dickens), "*Twelfth Night*" or "*The Merchant of Venice*" (Shakespeare), "*Silas Marner*" (George Eliot), "*Uncle Tom's Cabin*" (Mrs. Stowe, 1852), "*The Adventures of Tom Sawyer*" (Samuel Langhorne Clemens who wrote under the pseudonym, Mark Twain), "*Essays of Elia*" (Charles Lamb), "*Gulliver's Travels*" (Jonathan Swift, 1727) and even "*Don Quixote de la Mancha*" (Cervantes, 1605-1615)—used to be kept in the selection among many other children's adventures. Some books of

acknowledged excellence if widely read used to encourage a common understanding.

2. Some books specially had a place in the selection because later writers often made frequent allusion. Schools generally are unwilling to surrender those books. They are so well known, the teachers feel, that the best modern writing is inevitably full of allusions or references to their classic incidents and characters. To miss the force of these references is to miss so much pleasure. A large group of modern high school pupils are so far away from the atmosphere of books and academic culture that the study of the Bible, Homer, Bunyan (Pilgrim's Progress for its own English) would probably make little appeal to them. It goes without saying that they need not be set for the regular class courses. Their time could be more wisely spent upon books that make closer contact with their current life and thought. Never mind. In certain schools selected portions of these Classics may wisely be retained and in others none may be retained.

3. The literature selected should be distinctly good from the standpoint of style. It is not necessary that teachers in our high/senior secondary schools should be able to secure from their pupils a definition or an analysis of style, but it is necessary that the selections which are taken up in class should tend to develop a sense of this somewhat intangible quality.

   The reader of Charles Lamb's "*Essays of Elia*" inevitably comes to recognise, as he reads the subtle design and expertness of touch that shape, throughout, the high excellence of the whole. The Essays are largely autobiographical; they deal with mankind at large as seen through the medium of Lamb's own experiences and impressions. They present with exquisite humour and pathos, and in a brilliant and inimitable style, characters that the author has known: recollections of childhood, personal experiences (Dream Children), the productions of a playful or a melancholy fancy and general comments and criticisms. And when the same student turns to George Eliot's Silas Marner, he should be able to discern how different are the methods of the two authors, and to realize that this contrast is the natural result of the marked difference between the individualities of the two writers.

Through the study of carefully chosen books the pupil should gradually become familiar with some of the more easily discernible elements of style, such as correctness, beauty, force, definiteness, resonance and variety. Learning to perceive and recognize and evaluate these qualities in writing will bring him a high sense of satisfaction. He will gradually learn, too, to infuse some of them into his own writing.

4. The importance of a good style in writing suggests the inclusion in the course of certain literature that offers special and direct help in the current composition work. Some of the form of writing may be called the offspring of impulse and some other may have touch of mere mechanism. The one is as full of fancy as it is bare of facts; the other excludes all fancy, and is weighed down with facts. The one is all fire, the other, all ice; the one nothing but enthusiasm, extravagance, eccentricity, the other nothing but logical deductions. The form of writing, thus, will bear the stamp at times, or presence of mind, graceful manner or at other occasion a great animation in delivering personal sentiments. To expect the least, the study of certain poems may incite a class to undertake the writing of simple lyrics.

5. The trend to choice should generally be toward the classical writing (classics or famous writers). Almost everyone now-a-days is an avowed progressive, but many of us

are progressives with a certain well-defined qualifications of moderation. We wish to make haste slowly; to advance—but to advance with caution. Popularity is not synonymous with excellence.

We are hearing much current talk about the element of interest and we know that interest is the first essential to successful instruction. But there is a striking difference between the slowly aroused interest in something of permanent worth and the flash of transitory interest in something ephemeral. It is easier to read a modern popular story or fiction or a play than a play of Shakespeare's, but the value in the latter instance is likely to be proportionate to the difficulty.

6. The easy and the modern have their legitimate place, too, for the selections must be adjusted to the mind and taste of the pupils. With the admission of the large number of pupils many of whom are the first generation school-goers, even if from unlettered homes and with a vast and steadily increasing influx into all sorts of our high school population, there comes an insistent demand for readjustment. In certain quarters it is absolutely necessary that the English course be re-formed and re-graded. Reading selections must be then closely enough connected with the daily life and habitual thought of the pupil to attract his attention if it can ultimately offer him a hand for his climbing interest. It is this reason which justifies that the academic high school course should not ignore the modern note. Selections from modern themes reflect life as we are living it today. Its problems are our problems and its emotions, our emotions. Because of this the presentday writers voice their notions in the current magazines, or some such books which quickly win our interest and if they are wise writers, ultimately may enlarge our idealism. They redirect our thought to the fact that literature is forever in the making. But who are those

emerging authors who can become the accepted writers (classic) of tomorrow? The best periodical literature adventures, animals, environment, local movements, mystery, travel, games and sports and others is in close and vital touch with current thought and frequently it treats, in a lucid, stimulating, and systematic manner, the ideas that the high school pupil only vaguely perceives.

7. The acquired reputation or the historical significance of a particular book may suggest its inclusion. The pupil learns that the book has had a tremendous influence on world thought and on world life and he is glad that his attention has been directed to it. It is amazing and yet it is true that acclaimed great treatise, by and large, has been the stimulation of some moral principles. The pupils delight to see upon the stage of action, right in contest with wrong. The open and the straightforward methods generate constant sympathy. The writer does not bring in any abstract preaching. But the controlling technique of depiction is one that offers them guidance as much as builds their confidence. This is in line of proper education.

8. The English course should provide a variety of literary types. A true education encourages in all branches a versatility of tastes and offers a rather wide range of material. This variation and breadth are particularly desirable in the English course. To suggest a few groups: *(1)* the classics in translation, including Stories of the Old Testament, the themes from History and Mythology, Ancient Civilization (world over), *(2)* the Shakespeare group, *(3)* prose fiction, *(4)* essays and biography, *(5)* oratory and letters, *(6)* poetry. They are capable of various sub-divisions.

We must provide our pupils with all those different types of literature both vernacular and English if we want them to get a true idea of the richness and variety of the literary storehouse. More than that, each pupil ought to have a chance to test his individual taste in these various realms and to make his own choice—something that promises to him the highest inspiration and the keenest pleasure. True culture, the kinship among different civilisation comprises an acquaintance with the varied literary forms. If we want our pupils to know the best that has been known and thought in the world, we must guide them into these different realms. No wonder their choice will vary from time to time.

9. The students should be introduced to literature that displays a variety of moods. The question of diverse moods is different from the question of diverse types, but not altogether independent of it. We do not like continued tragedy or comedy; we yearn for a change. In making our selection we must welcome, to our course, such various elements as the mystic, the fanciful, the whimsical, the idealistic, the realistic, the supramental, the spiritual, the tragic, the comic, and all the manifold phases of humanity that the great masters have portrayed. It is specially desirable that we should not ignore the humorous.

SECONDARY AND SENIOR SECONDARY: ENGLISH SYLLABUS

For the first time a notion of a syllabus for the English course for classes IX and X is sighted, in the teaching materials in the course entitled, 'Interact in English' (CBSE-1993). I shall clear my point gradually.

We have been having, for decades, English books containing reading materials of different types prepared in the form of anthology where a team of Indian experts happen to edit the book/books. In the selection of beautiful and profitable writings which make the anthologies, experts working in different parts of the country had extended their encouragement and all possible help. At such selection of course materials for the XI and XII classes—the Core and

Elective, even the involvement of the Department of Materials Production, CIEFL, Hyderabad and NCERT seem laudable. Grateful acknowledgements for permission to use copyright, materials are offered: as also copyright permission for some materials are sought for. The writers, whose writings are included in the course selection belong to different countries of the world, India being one of them.

For the Senior Secondary Elective English Course, two anthologies of contemporary prose and one anthology of poems are prescribed (1994). These publications have been in use since 1978 till today. Besides, the above reading materials, the syllabus comprise grammar and composition. The Core course for Class XII English, comprise books for detailed and non-detailed study along with workbook experience to enable the student to use English for purpose of communication and expression. The course (core) aims to enable a senior secondary student to use English effectively as a library language. The development of sophisticated writing skills like note-making, summarising have been stressed, as the thrust of the syllabus in Class XII is on the development of these skills. Students competence in writing with ease and facility is the primary aim, as "equipped" with such skills they will survive in the "world of tomorrow."

The senior secondary Elective English Course is aiming at developing mature reading at the intermediate stage where a thorough wide-ranging exposure to a variety of styles and registers is planned. The initial commitment called for different types of reading material at an appropriate level of difficulty and challenge. The thrust of the course is on pieces which have a pronounced literary bias. The book contains passages which bring in a variety of themes in the field of face and fiction, description and reflection, travel and biography.

The editors have placed reading comprehension with a view to developing thought-getting and critical understanding along with literary interpretation, inference and evaluation. The composition exercise that emanate from the text lists writing tasks which are primarily imaginative in nature and involve analysing, interpreting, reviewing and commenting on the text. The poems (Elective English) '*Eternal Lines-A Book of Poems*' in the Anthology have to be treated for two distinct purposes. On the one hand the poems have been arranged chronologically to enable the student to note the development of English poetry from Shakespeare's times to ours and to be aware of the living tradition that it represents. On the other hand, apart from exemplifying some of best poetry written in UK, India, the USA and Chile, the anthology includes representative pieces from several important poetic genres like the sonnet, the lyric and the dramatic monologue. Most of the poems in this anthology are rich in ideas, in sentiments, and in human appeal. The Board of Editors provided some vital suggestions regarding steps in the teaching of a poem. This of course could be debated, since the choice of methodology may best be left to the experienced and resourceful teacher, who believes that the reading of a poem is essentially a joy, and a 'recollection in tranquility'.

We come back to the basic question. What is a Syllabus? On what primary elements or constructs should the English Language syllabus framing be understood? "Syllabus" is not 'books' alone; nor is a syllabus, a collection of tasks/activities. Syllabus comprises materials of study, no doubt, but the basic principles behind the preparation of syllabus, must be probed in first.

In language teaching, as in other fields, new movements often begin as reactions to old ones. Their origins, that is, lie in a discontent with an existing state of affairs. Most of us are familiar with the structurally competent but communicatively incompetent student. One understands that the ability to manipulate the structures of the language correctly is only a part of what is involved in learning a language. There is 'something else' that needs to be learned and this 'something else' involves the ability to be appropriate, to know the right thing to say at the right time.

A syllabus is in general terms a 'list of items we wish to teach; and if we see our main aim as being the teaching of structures then it is entirely natural that our syllabuses as 'lists of items to teach', should be lists of structures. This is more or less what, until recent times, syllabuses have been. With the mastery of structures, it is seen, that a student is unable to perform the communicative task simply because, we have never considered items, say, asking something from somebody, or in more general terms, 'requesting services', as part of our teaching content. If a syllabus is a list of items we wish to teach, and if we are prepared to see language learning as a question of mastering not only structures but also 'meanings' or 'uses', then our syllabuses must list items of 'meaning' or 'use' as well as 'items of structure'.

But how does one list 'meanings' or 'uses'? This is one of the problems which a team of experts convened by the Council of Europe in 1971 set out to answer. It became necessary to develop a system of categories by means of which it would be possible to specify the communicative needs of a learner. Now communicative functions are in broad terms, the uses to which we put language. The categories of 'communicative function' have come to be known, for the sake of brevity, as functions. They do relate to some extent, to grammatical categories, yet forms of expression need not remain restricted to a single grammar form alone.

We have come a long way from the traditional method of selecting readymade writings (production of writers) and preparing some anthologies (prose and poetry) which the experts passed on as comprising our syllabus for secondary and senior secondary classes. The question is still alive. What is the basis of syllabus designing in English in our school curriculum? The older approaches tended to emphasise 'form' (structural syllabus) at the expense of 'meaning'; but now it may be other way round. When students were taught the forms of the language, they did not learn the meanings or communicative use of these forms. Nowadays, things are different. We start from a semantic syllabus, which categorises the language in terms of meaning and communicative functions and we relate the forms to these meanings. We are getting a good deal better at teaching students to use language forms in ways appropriate to their purposes. But are we sure that we are doing a good job of helping them to learn the forms themselves? We doubt if there is such a thing as a single syllabus (structural or communicative or any other). In fact, there are various syllabuses, corresponding to the various points of view from which language can be described, and a language programme may contain elements drawn from some or all of them. (Michael Swan: *False beginners*. From, Communication in the classroom. Ed. by Keith Johnson & Keith Morrow. Longman, 1986). These syllabuses include the following:

A Phonological Syllabus: Examples of items that might be included how to pronounce/Q/, how to distinguish /S/&/Z/; weak forms: contrastive high pitch.

A Lexical Syllabus: Examples of possible items: tall, guitar, relax, dashboard.

A Structural Syllabus: Possible items: prepositions with points of time, 'the present progressive' with future reference; some and any.

A Situational Syllabus: Possible items: what to say when shopping, how to answer the phone.

A Topic Syllabus: Possible items: the language used to talk about marriage and divorce, the parts of a car.

A National Syllabus: Possible items: how to refer to points of time, how to talk about the future, how to refer to the instrument with which an action is performed.

A Stylistic Syllabus: Possible items: levels of politeness degrees of formality, poetic word order.

A Functional Syllabus: Possible items: how to warn; how to express enthusiastic appreciation; how to borrow things.

A Cultural Background Syllabus: Possible items: British humour, the American electoral system, nursery rhymes.

A Discourse Syllabus: Possible items: the use of intonation as a floor-holding device, how to break into a conversation boundary markers in speech and writing.

A Rhetorical Syllabus: Possible items: summarising, writing business letter, organizing an essay.

On the framing of the English course giving equal importance to each of these syllabuses in all kinds of course is next to impossible. Normally, the first seven syllabuses contain essential components of most language teaching programmes.

Before beginning any teaching operation we list the items we wish our students to learn. In a structural syllabus, we might as a first stage list the grammatical items such as, 'verb constructions', 'articles' or, 'noun phrase constructions' and so on. The essential job of grading and combining the structures into sequences for teaching would constitute the second stage of operation.

But when we consider semantic as opposed to structural syllabus design, one further step is required to convert a syllabus inventory into a syllabus. This is because semantic syllabus inventories contain not one but many lists-not just structures but functions, settings, topics, role and several other types of categories as well. We clearly cannot devise a programme to teach language associated with each of these lists in turn—neither together, nor in a sequence either. We have to select one of these types of item as our 'unit of organisation'. We may decide that each teaching unit of our course should cover one function. This will then be called a 'functional syllabus'. Such a syllabus should of course not ignore the other types of list on the inventory. We would have to ensure that the language presented under the various functional headings took account of the settings, topics, and role. We might well have chosen the setting (in a shop, in the library, at the station) or the topic (education festivals, travel, a visit to the zoo etc.) and so on. What is most baffling in this task is how to decide which type of item to choose as the basis for syllabus organization to suit the characteristics of our learners. This point has not received much theoretical attention.

The question of 'unit of organisation' opens up the possibility for syllabus with varied units of organisation. Let us begin with one type of item as our organising principle; we need not change the orientation of the course too often and too hurriedly; but there is no reason why we should not vary the unit of organisation within the course.

Keith Johnson refers to a brilliant combination of procedures: "In many teaching situations, for example, an attractive possibility is to follow a series of functional units in which a variety of grammatical items is met, with structural units which focus attention on these items and relate them to the grammatical system as a whole. Similarly, there may be good pedagogic reasons for concentrating in some parts of a course on the language appropriate to chosen setting and on others in language in relation to functions. We might dub this type of syllabus, 'multi-dimensional' to distinguish it from the 'unidimensional' syllabus in which the unit of organisation does not change at all." Our aim is to teach communicative ability, and this may lead us at the syllabus design level to specify and organise our teaching content in a semantic way. That the semantic syllabus is to lead to a destination is not judged by how it is organised but also in terms of its methodology.

We have to look at the task of foreign language learning from the point of view of the learner. Why learners are in fact learning a foreign language? There must be some clear relevance to their needs in using the foreign language. Here arises the problem to design such a programme when the needs are not easily specified or may be extremely varied. Language learning at school level must begin by being 'instrumental' to some extent but also must base itself on certain fundamental broader educational grounds. It should be understood that we are not ignoring the needs-oriented teaching of the uses of foreign language at school level but we are widening its scope in a much desirable direction.

❐

11

Teaching of Grammar and Translation

The teaching of grammar, has been a vexed question for a very long time. If there are many advocates in favour of its inclusion in the curriculum, there are equally many critics who strongly oppose any grammar teaching in schools. There are varying views too of the amount and type of grammar to be taught—inductive grammar, functional grammar, formal grammar, little grammar or no grammar. Modern researches in linguistics and language teaching have brought to light one very important fact *i.e.* that in order to understand, speak or read English, what is required is actual use of the language. No specific grammar programme is necessary. A new language can be learnt easily without the knowledge of any formal grammar as such. In fact, the earliest emergence of formal grammar in England was found as late as the sixteenth century with the work of William Bullokar (1580) and the seventeenth century with the work of John Wallis (1653). But that does not mean that English literature did not exist before that. Some of the greatest literary work *i.e.* the work of Chaucer, Milton and various other poets and dramatists were written long before a formal grammar was formulated. In India, the earliest traces of grammar were found in Panini's *Astadhyaya* in 400 BC, while among the ancient Greeks, formal grammar made its appearance in the writings of Aristotle and Plato. But in England, it made its appearance much later. This shows that knowledge of formal grammar is not essential for reading and writing good English. The same holds true when a comprehensive English course is planned for Indian schools. The different aspects of language teaching *i.e.* speaking, understanding, reading and writing, need no formal training in grammar. Hence, formal teaching of grammar should be completely avoided during the earlier years of teaching English. But a time comes when acquaintance with some grammatical terms, and their usage becomes essential. This too should be attempted only after children have built up a fairly good working vocabulary and numerous sentences about their actions.

REASONS FOR TEACHING GRAMMAR

Some grammar teaching becomes inevitable in the higher classes in the secondary schools. But at no time is it necessary to let the children pore over detailed analysis of sentences and long parsing exercises. Such exercises are a relic of old Latin teaching, and do not have much value in teaching language in the modern times. In fact it is such vague and complicated exercises as are responsible for the horror and hatred that most children feel towards grammar.

The true nature of grammar and its place in the teaching of any language is not clearly understood very often by teachers. One must not forget that grammar is taught for the sake of language, and is not an end in itself. The nature of grammar and its relation to language have been summed up clearly by Morris, as follows:

1. The foundation of a living language is the spoken and not the written form.
2. English has developed as a language on its own lines, and cannot be forced to conform with any earlier language rules.
3. A living language is not static but in a state of flux and change.

4. The function of words or word order is more important to language than inflextions or collocations.

5. The example and observation of these examples are more to important than grammatical rules.

6. Grammar does not lay down rules for any language to be followed. It merely observes and records the language. If it is customary to use a particular idiom, grammar notes the trend. It has no power to stop it, for *e.g.*, the changing form of writing addresses and letters according to the American style.

7. The true unit of any language is not the word, but the word group.

The rules of grammar hence are not divinely established laws that must be followed under any circumstances. These rules merely explain the use of language, and record the trend that the language is taking.

PRESENT POSITION OF GRAMMAR IN LANGUAGE TEACHING

Why do we teach grammar at all? What is its place in the syllabus?

First and foremost, it must be remembered that grammar is not a separate subject, nor it a separate division of English work. If it is so marked in the syllabus or timetable, it is for our convenience. It is an essential part of the English course, but not separate subject. It helps us to get the "feel" of the language. Many of us try and dispense with it altogether. But it must be taught mainly for the sake of composition and reading. Grammar is a study of the language as we hear it; the study of the behaviour of words, word-groups and changes in meaning of words. Thus, Grammar is not a subject itself, but a very useful handmade to composition and reading. It is no longer an abstract subject but a useful means of correcting faulty speech or composition. Hence, the modern belief is that all

Grammar teaching should be linked up with reading and composition lesson.

Only theoretical knowledge is not advisable. This has always been the great trouble with Grammar teaching. Instead of being an incidental in the English course, it has been allowed to swell to unnatural proportions of assumed ridiculous importance. It has been allowed to become a law into itself.

The important point to remember is that Grammar must always *follow*. It must always be behind reading and writing. A child's learning of language is gradual and not by rule. Similarly, students should be guided to "discover" a new form of the language. This is the inductive form of teaching Grammar.

Characteristics of Grammar

The definitions involve the following characteristics of grammar.

1. Grammar is the theory of a language.
2. It is the study of the organization of words into sentences which is based on certain rules.
3. Every language has its own grammatical nouns.
4. Grammar has not the code rules, it is like etiquette and table manners of speaking and writing a language.
5. English grammar was developed and written on the basis of Latin Grammar.
6. Grammar is a study of characteristics and specialities of a language. It has been made in order to establish the rules and principles which are followed by the speakers and writers.
7. Grammar is a major component of language which establishes the relationship between words.

8. Grammar presents the facts and rules of a language, arranged into certain categories and slated in the form of general rules.
9. A language is constituted in a meaning arrangements of words and sentences by its Grammar.
10. Grammar has three different meanings:
    (a) The first meaning of grammar is the set of formal pattern of arranging words of a language.
    (b) The second meaning of grammar is the branch of linguistic science and analytical aspect of a language.
    (c) The third meaning of grammar is linguistic etiquette or norms.

Objectives of Teaching Grammar

The main objectives of teaching grammar are enumerated as follows:

1. To develop a scientific attitude about the language.
2. To develop students' insight into the structures of English language.
3. To enable the pupils to express their ideas logically and correctly in speech and writing.
4. To teach grammar as a rule-governed behaviour and not as mere rote learning.
5. To enable the pupils to develop their understanding about the rules of English grammar through use and practice of its structures.
6. To develop their mental abilities of reasoning and correct observation.
7. To enable the students to assimilate the correct patterns of the language without rote memorisation.

Place of Grammar in School Curriculum

With the introduction of Direct Method, grammar is fast disappearing from school curriculum. In spite of the demerits of grammar, the education of grammar is essential. The place it should occupy should have the following main features:

(1) The descriptive grammar which emphasises on function of language should be taught, because in the words of Ballard, *"Formal grammar fails to provide a general mental training, does not enable teachers to eradicate solecism, does not aid in compositions and takes up time which could much more profitably be devoted to the study of literature"*.

(2) It should be taught incidently and informally at the early stage. At the middle stage, inductive or deductive method is more useful. At the higher level, it can be taught in the traditional method.

(3) It should occupy a secondary place. It should be a means to an end, not the end itself.

(4) It should follow the language. CE Eckersley says, *"The rules of grammar are like the laws of nature. The laws were not made for nature to obey, but are simply a few facts which wise men have observed as to the way nature acts"*.

(5) Teaching of grammar should only start when pupils acquire some command over the language.

(6) During the first year only function of the word and the way they are used should be taught. It includes: subject and predicate, subject and verb; use of small and capital letters; use of full stop, comma and question-mark; singular and plural; simple present, past and future tenses; use of first, second and third persons; genders. During second and third years, sentence-pattern, phrase-pattern,

structural words and the ways in which English uses a few inflexions, should be taught. At the senior stage, these should be followed coupled with analysis, synthesis, direct and indirect narration, transformation; compound and difficult sentences.

Types of Grammar

Grammar is evolving as language evolves. So there are different types of grammar. Some of the important types of grammar are as follows:

(1) ***Descriptive Grammar or Functional Grammar:*** It possesses the new concept of grammar. In it, the main emphasis is on the functional side of language. In other words, it describes the behaviour of language. It overcomes the limitation of perspective grammar because it changes along with the changes in the language.

(2) ***Perspective Grammar:*** It is also called formal or theoretical grammar. It is the old traditional grammar. In it, the main emphasis is on rules and forms. It ties language with rules. Its limitation is that it does not consider 'change in language', whereas change in rules is must.

(3) ***Scholarly Traditional Grammar:*** This type of grammar was developed by the scholars of universities. In developing it, they used bibliographic references, critical evolution of the work of predecessors and thorough documentation by citations from English literature. The weakness of this type of grammar is diversity.

(4) ***Structural Grammar:*** CC Fries an American linguist was the founder of this type of grammar. This grammar emphasises on structures of sentences. The descriptive linguistics are much influenced by it.

(5) ***Transformational-Generative Grammar:*** According to this type of grammar, sentences are of two types: *(i)* basic

sentences, and *(ii)* transformed sentences. Basic sentences cannot be derived from other sentences, *e.g.*, "He is going." The transformed sentences are derived from the basic sentences, *e.g.*, "Is he going?" This grammar is in a developing stage and perhaps in future will give a systematic syntax of English.

Importance and Merits of Teaching Grammar: There are some scholars who advocate the case of grammar. LA Gordon says, "Language is the vehicle of our thoughts and feelings and of our stories, whether true or not and grammar is the machinery by which that vehicle is set in motion." The following are the merits of grammar:

(1) Language is a complex system. It must have logic, a grammar is, behind it.

(2) So far correct expression in a language is concerned, grammar is essential.

(3) Grammar teaching is essential if we want to proceed from concrete to abstract.

(4) It helps in developing many mental abilities such as: reasoning, observation and concentration.

(5) It gives an insight into the structure of the language.

(6) It is a systematised knowledge of a language.

(7) It provides a criteria for judging the correctness of language.

(8) Its importance in writing is undebatable.

(9) It helps in writing correctly.

Limitations of Teaching Grammar: At present times, grammar is losing its importance. Scholars have freely criticised it. P Gurrey views, "In secondary schools, the use of parsing and full analysis is a waste of time compared to the effectiveness of many other exercises." Holiday and his colleagues condemned it by saying, "Much of English grammar taught within the old method was pedantic, or archaic, even erroneous." According to Jesperson, "Grammar is not a set of stiff dogmatic percepts, according to which somethings are correct and others absolutely wrong." This criticism is due to the following demerits of grammar:

1. It does not provide ideas, and language without ideas is lifeless.
2. It deals with only a part of language because it does not deal with idioms, phrases, proverbs, fluency, articulation, vocabulary, colloquial expressions, and power of speech.
3. It does not include thought and expression in its domain.
4. It does not include the formation of paragraphs, the rhythm of expression, and the styled speaking and writing.

Principles of Teaching a Grammar: The following principles should be noted before planning of grammar lessons:

1. Students do not understand abstractions. Hence, we should not begin with abstract statements of a grammatical principle.

2. Grammar lessons should begin with language. It must correlate speech, in which a sentence is a unitary whole with reading. After the students have listened to it, try to guide them to deduce the pattern that we want them to use.

3. In the beginning stages, a separate grammar book need not be introduced. Let the pupils unconsciously absorb grammatical items as contained in the reader.

4. It is the meaning which matters most. So attention should be paid on meaning of the structure rather than on grammatical points unless they are interfering with the communication of meaning.

5. Encourage the students to make up their own examples of what we want them to use so that every student could listen to as many correct usages as possible.

6. The teacher should present progressively graded matter for the students to be acquired by production and repetition.

7. Teach such grammatical terminology as is useful and necessary, though in due course of time, the students would require more.

8. Grammar should not be taught as an intellectual exercise of the pupils but the aim should be to make them skilful users of the language. Teach the students to use the structures of English correctly rather than how to label them.

9. According to McGregor, "If we are to teach the grammar of English realistically and truthfully, then we must, as soon as possible, help our pupils to understand the concept of "idiom in language" because all languages are different in the total means which they employ to convey meaning. We are not concerned here to know why different languages do so but how they do so.

10. Learning grammar is like learning masonary or carpentry. Knowledge of the names of the tools is not useful for these skills. The learner must know their use. So is with learning the grammar. Students must be able to use the pattern skilfully and build up their own structures.

Methods of Teaching Grammar

The various methods advocated for the teaching of grammar are:

1. ***The Traditional Method:*** In this method a text-book on grammar is used. It contains definitions, rules, examples,

and exercises. The teacher tells a definition, or a rule. For example, he says, "A Noun is the name of a person, place or thing." He gives examples of nouns. Then, he refers to an exercise and asks the pupils to point out the nouns in it. The pupils have to memorise the definition of noun. This very procedure is followed for teaching other parts of speech. When they are well learnt by the pupils, the teacher introduces them to rules regarding the change of masculine nouns into feminine nouns, transformation and analysis of sentences, change of voice of narration, etc.

2. ***The Informal Method:*** This method advocates the teaching of grammar not by rules but by usages. By continuous practice of using words while speaking, reading and writing, grammar can be learnt. This method proves useful at the early stage when pupils are taught orally.

   According to Suri and Bhardwaj:

   > "The informal method connotes teaching of no grammatical rules, but explaining correct usage informally during correction work. The method is a necessity in the early stages when the pupils have not mastered enough of vocabulary and are yet baffling with speech."

3. ***The Inductive-Deductive Method:*** This method is thought to be the best method because it follows some educational principles. As a matter of fact, Inductive-Deductive method is used to teach science. Since grammar is a science of language, it is successfully used for teaching grammar. Some grammarians think that both inductive and deductive are difficult methods. But it will not be appropriate to treat them as such, as pointed out by Thompson and Wyatt "Even when the facts are discovered inductively, the knowledge acquired has to be applied deductively, or it is apt to be forgotten for lack of use."

4. ***The Incidental or Correlational Method:*** In this method grammar is taught incidently. This is done during the teaching of text-book, doing translation work, or writing composition. Complex structures are explained and the grammatical implications are taught simultaneously. But sometimes these things interfere with the normal course of teaching a particular topic, because sometimes there is an unnecessary divergence. "However, this method is very suitable, as a supplementary to the Inductive-Deductive Method. After the rules of grammar have been taught, in the grammar period, reference at the proper occasion may be made in the intensive reading or composition period for purposes of further drill and application."

Inductive Process: Inductive means to proceed from observations to law, from simple to complex. For teaching grammar inductively the following steps should be followed:

1. ***Presentation of Examples and Illustrations:*** The teacher presents examples and illustrations in a systematic order, so that they may lead to a generalisation. For example, if the teacher wants to teach how the active voice is changed into the passive voice. He can write the following sentences on the black board.

The cat killed a rat.	Rat was killed by the cat.
He forget the book.	The book was forgotten by him.
Radha sang a song.	A song was sung by Radha.

2. ***Analysis of Examples:*** The teacher helps the pupils to analyse the two types of sentences. He asks them to point out the subject, verb and predicate. He asks them to compare the positions of the subject and the object in both the types of sentences. He asks them to point out the change in the verbs. In the end, he asks them to tell all the changes that they find in the second type of sentences.

3. ***Generalisation:*** When the pupils understand the changes mentioned above, they themselves come to certain conclusions. In other words, they come to a generalisation, which is as follows:

   (i) The object becomes the subject.

   (ii) The subject becomes the object and preceded by the preposition.

   (iii) The form of the verb changes. The Past Indefinite (kill, forget and sang) changes into the Participle form.

4. ***Verification of the Rules:*** The teacher presents new examples for the verification of the above rules. In case, there are any exceptions, the teacher helps the pupils to discover them.

5. ***The Rules:*** After the students have pointed out the changes, the teacher tells them that these changes form the rules for changing the Active into the Passive.

6. ***Practice in the Change of Voice:*** The teacher gives ample practice to the pupils in the change of voice by asking them to give examples. These examples or sentences are changed from active into passive or *vice versa*.

TEACHING OF TRANSLATION

Translation is the meaning of English words or phrases and sentences, taught by means of word for word into the mother-tongue. Translation lays stress upon reading. Without reading 'a word for word' translation into the mother-tongue is not possible.

Translation can be used in two ways:

1. As a method and

2. As a skill.

Translation as a teaching method has been condemned. As a skill, it has its own importance. Here teaching of translation deals with translation as a skill. In fact, translation is a skill which involves a high level of understanding of one language and good command of the other. It demands a grasp of the meaning and spirit of an English passage and must know the appropriate phraseology to convey the same in the mother-tongue.

Types of Translation: There are two types of translation:

1. Word translation
2. Sentence translation

These both types of translation can be:

1. From English to mother-tongue
2. From mother-tongue to English
3. Retranslation, *i.e.*, from English to mother-tongue and from mother-tongue to English.

One another type of division is:

1. Oral and
2. Written

It is advisable not to use word translation. Also, the translation should not be from English to mother-tongue at an early stage, because it hinders the development of new language habit. At the later stage, it can be introduced. The oral translation should precede written translation.

Exercise for Translation: The teacher can have the following for translation:

(1) Structures and

(2) Sentences with:

(a) different tenses,

(b) comparative and supperlative degrees,

(c) relative pronouns,

(d) active and passive voices,

(e) appropriate prepositions,

(f) words like however, although, nevertheless, yet, though, not withstanding,

(g) direct and indirect narrations,

(3) Idioms and phrases,

(4) Passages.

Principles of Teaching Translation: It is based on the following principles:

1. In the process of interpretation the foreign phraseology is assimilated.

2. Translation interprets foreign phraseology best.

3. The structure of a foreign language is best learnt when compared and contrasted with that of the mother-tongue.

Significance of Translation: The significance of translation is obvious from the following:

(i) It helps the teacher to test pupils' understanding of an English word. According to Rybum, "There is no better test of knowledge of English than translation from the mother-tongue into English."

(ii) It serves as exercise in comprehension.

(iii) It brings out the differences of grammatical structures of sentences in English and mother-tongue.

(iv) There is much need of translation of books on humanities and science. The skill of translation learnt at school can be of great help in this regard.

(v) It makes students learn English by understanding its differences from the mother-tongue.

Procedure for Planning a Grammar Lesson: The Functional grammar is taught through structural readers and not through the grammar book. In the structural readers important grammatical points are mentioned for the purpose of teaching. So, every lesson based on the structural syllabi aims at teaching functional grammar.

For planning a grammar lesson, therefore, the structure to be taught is selected from the reader itself. Grammar lessons are taught as a part of the reading lessons. The following steps are followed to teach a grammar lesson:

1. ***Introduction:*** The teacher tests the previous knowledge of the students through appropriate questions on the previous structures learned by them. In this way, he is proceeding from known to unknown. Then he introduces the new structure with the help of examples.

2. ***Objectives of the Lesson:*** The teacher writes the behavioural objectives for teaching a particular grammar lesson.

3. ***Statement of Aim:*** After having introduced the new structure in appropriate situations, the teacher states his aim in unambiguous language.

4. ***Practice of the Structure:*** The teacher then organises practice drills which are mainly oral. The use of blackboard, flash cards and substitution tables can be made for this purpose. Structures should be used in as many new situations as possible by changing the vocabulary words.

5. ***Presentation:*** The teacher presents a few sentences using the new structure in a variety of situations. The students try to follow the meaning of the structure by observing its use in different situations by the teacher. Then they try to formulate their own adhoc rules about the use of a given structure. The job of the teacher, is just to lead the students skilfully to the desired grammatical point. Through imitation and repetition the pupils grasp the correct use of the structure. The use of mother-tongue is not a ban in the teaching of grammar. If needed, it can be used.

6. ***Home Assignment:*** At the end, students are given a few exercises to practise the new structure at their homes.

On the basis of the above mentioned steps lessons on grammar can be planned. But the modern trend is to teach grammar not as a separate subject but along with the reading lessons.

Steps for Teaching Grammar: The teaching of grammar should be started in the first year of the English course as soon as pupils acquire some measure of command over the language. But the grammar taught to them should in no case be formal grammar which should be gradually introduced only when they are in the third year or class VIII. The purpose of teaching English during the first two years is to give them a command over the basic structures of the language. Hence, in the first year the grammar they are taught should be in the form of function of words and the way they are used. Care should be taken that they do not get lost in the rules of grammar and definitions of grammatical terms. They should be made familiar with the general rules of grammar through imitation, practice, and repetitions. For example, they can be taught the agreement of subject and verb, if they are made to imitate the teacher, practice and repeat sentences such as:—

This is a ball.

These are balls.

This is a book.

Those are books.

He is a boy.

They are boys.

The students of English language must have the knowledge of the following:

1. The sentence
2. Subject and Predicate
3. The phrase and the clause
4. Parts of Speech
5. Gender
6. Number
7. The uses of the Tenses.
8. Active/Passive
9. Transformation
10. Idioms
11. Figures of speech, etc.

LESSON PLAN

Teaching Grammar

Date.... Topic *Pronoun* Pd-II

Class VII B

General Objectives: The following are the general objectives of teaching Grammar.

1. To provide the knowledge and understanding of the various aspects of grammar.

2. To develop the abilities and skills among students to speak and write correct English language.

3. To enable students to use the rules of grammar in speaking and writing English.

4. To increase the interest of students in English language.

5. To develop the linguistic ability among students and use in their own expression.

Specific Objectives: The following are the specific objectives of teaching Pronoun in English grammar.

1. To acquaint the students with the term pronoun.

2. To provide the meaning of pronoun in relation to noun.

3. To define the term pronoun.

4. To identify the pronouns in the English sentences.

5. To use the pronoun in writing and speaking sentences in English language.

Previous Knowledge: The students have the knowledge and understanding of the term noun. The students are able to identify the nouns in a sentence and make use in writing their own sentences.

❐

12

Techniques of Teaching, Writing and Composition

Here are given the techniques of teaching a language in very brief manner.

Narration is one of the most important devices for oral communication, and makes the subject of language interesting and easy to grasp. All new material cannot be elicited from the student and although questions help in drawing out the pupils and arresting their attention, narration according to Panton, is an art in itself. It aims at presenting to the pupils, through the medium of speecn, clear, vivid, interesting ordered sequences of events in such a way that their minds reconstruct these happenings. They live in the imagination through these experiences recounted as either spectators or possibly as participants.

Listening is an important step towards language learning and hence a teacher of English can exploit narration to the fullest extent to encourage listening. Narration should, made as vivid and imaginative as possible. It should always be done in an enthusiastic manner. Narration is an art that every teacher should master. Language is the medium through which narration is done. Hence, a language teacher should make plentiful use of this device. Certain points should be kept in mind with regard to narration.

1. *Story Telling.* It is the best form of narration. The stories should be suited to the age and standard of the children.
2. Narration should be made interesting by the use of handy illustrations such as metaphors and similes relating to verbal experiences with which children are familiar. Such illustrations add to the effectiveness of narration.
3. The teacher should himself be interested in what he is narrating and for this the subject matter and the purpose of narration should be quite clear to the teacher.
4. During narration, there should be proper interaction and gestures. A dramatic form of story-telling is of immense value to teachers of younger children.
5. Proper sequence of events must be maintained. A teacher should not jump events and come back to them later.
6. Narration should always be natural and oral and not read from a book or magazine.
7. The teacher should narrate as a model and the children should follow with their own experiences.
8. Children are always more interesting in action and sense impressions, hence long descriptions should be avoided. The narrator can be made as one of the characters in the story.

Illustrations: These can be in the form of models, charts, pictures etc. which help in the explanation of difficult ideas by making an appeal to different senses. They stimulate interest and arouse the curiosity of children. Variety can also be introduced by the teacher introducing personal experiences into the explanation *e.g.,* in teaching a poem like "Somebody's Mother", personal experience of snow or rain can be narrated. In explaining "Daffodils", personal experiences of a field of flowers can be brought in. So also in processions easy and simple illustrations help in comprehending the difficult. Illustrations may be non-verbal or concrete and verbal. Non-verbal illustration may be in the form of models objects, specimen, pictures and photographs, diagrams, graphs, maps, charts or black-board drawings. Verbal may be in the form of descriptions, analogies, similes, word pictures etc.

For lower classes, concrete illustrations are always better. However, illustrations are a means and not the end of teaching. There should not be too many illustrations, so that the real objective of the lesson is lost. Illustrations should serve as an aid to the teacher.

Questioning: The art of good questioning can serve as one of the most important devices of teaching, as used in learning, teaching and testing. It has been effectively pointed out that the success and efficacy of teaching largely depends on our skill of questioning. The teacher who never questions, never teaches. In fact, questioning is the key to all educative activity.

Questions may be of different types:

1. Preliminary or introductory questions, asked in the beginning of a lesson.
2. Recapitulatory questions for testing how much the students have understood towards the end of lesson.
3. Developing or teaching questions, asked during the presentation stage. Here, each question is a step forward in the final construction of knowledge and facts. Vague questions should be avoided.

The skill of framing the questions too is important. Questions, that contain their own answer should be avoided, as also too long questions. Yes-no type questions or those that ask too much of the students, should not be attempted too often.

Self-Study and Assignments: Although a major amount of teaching-learning is done in classroom situations, assignments encourage the children to plan and perform their work independently.

It does not have the restrictive atmosphere of the classroom, and many a time a child may discover the area of his interest and pursue this to acquire considerable knowledge. Self study develops the moral and intellectual qualities of self-reliance, self-direction and initiative in grouping unaided with the problems arising from the work. Assignment also fosters the habits of reading regularly that are important from the point or view of adult life. Also the parents are made aware of what the child is doing in school. One of the biggest drawbacks of this method is that often there is no communication between different subject teachers, and hence on some days there may be too much work and on others, too little homework.

Substitution Tables: Substitution is a process by which any model sentence may be multiplied indefinitely by substituting or any of its words, other words of the same grammatical family.

The first thing to be done in preparing a substitution table is to select a model sentence, because it has been felt that study of a word apart from its sentence does not help in forming correct linguistic habits. The sentence is the most complete unit of thought. The substitution table can be arranged as follows:

The purse			the table
The cup	was	under	the chair
The pen	is	on	the book
The pencil			the bed
The nail		......	the floor

Model Sentence: Some particular idiom or construction is taken and a sentence is framed, using it. This sentence must be grammatically correct *e.g.* use of the preposition "on" with a number of sentences based on this model can be constructed. Each model sentence must illustrate some basic structure. The aim is to enable students to make many grammatically correct sentences with the model sentence using different content words. The correct use of the structure gives a sense of achievement to the pupil, which is psychologically satisfying, thus providing the right motivation for further learning. Substitution tables are very useful in fixing the right sentence patterns in the minds of the pupils. They provide good drill work and practice to the pupils.

There are two types of substitution tables:

(a) ***Simple Substitution Tables:*** Simple substitution tables which embody only one structure pattern and various content words *e.g.* the model shown above. In this table, the student can select any words from the first column to the last, and yet frame grammatically, correct sentence.

(b) ***Complex Substitution Tables:*** In this type of substitution table, two or more structures are presented simultaneously, and the student has to make the right choice in order to frame grammatically correct sentences for *e.g.,*

Does				school	yesterday	
	he					
Did		go	to	play	today	?
	she					
Will				study	tomorrow	

Advantages

(1) Substitution tables are very useful for providing drill word to larger classes, as many students can be attended to by the teacher at the same time.

(2) They are very useful in fixing the right structure pattern in grammar lessons.

(3) They help to focus the attention of the children on the black-board, and hence are idea teaching-aids for larger classes.

(4) They are psychologically stimulating to the pupils as they enable them to make grammatically correct sentences with minimum help from the teacher.

Thus substitution tables can be effectively used as teaching, testing and fixing devices.

WRITING

Writing plays a very important part in the life of an individual and is one of the most useful skills learnt in school. Hence, it is essential that teachers should pay due attention to this aspect of education. Writing work has two aspects, penmanship or simple handwriting and a form of exercise in learning the language, *i.e.* written composition. We shall deal with the first aspect which is of great importance to the teacher, as writing reflects the character of the person. It is teacher's duty to guide the children to acquire a good and legible handwriting.

Writing is now more or less a regular feature of the school work. However, the importance of written work is not the same for all pupils because written work cannot be compared with oral work for making sound progress in language learning. One expresses one's thoughts and opinions mainly through writing which is a valuable means of self-expression. Consequently, children should daily be encouraged to write at least a few of their ideas and experiences. Writing is an essential aid to expression and should be taught so that it becomes a smooth and efficient means of expressing thought.

Qualities of Good Handwriting

The qualities of a good handwriting are:

(i) Distinctiveness : Each letter should have a characteristic form of its own.

(ii) Simplicity : It should not have any unnecessary flourishes.

(iii) Spacing : There should be no overcrowding of letters or words.

(iv) Uniformity : Whatever style the individual adopts should be uniform in size, spacing and alignment, specially straight strokes.

(v) Speed : Writing should not be laboured but should have reasonable speed and fluency.

Method of Teaching Writing

It is assumed that before a child begins to write in English he must have had certain writing practice in his mother tongue. Hence, he knows some manipulation of the first hand fingers. But it is desirable that the teacher should give some training in penmanship. F.G. French suggests the following steps to encourage a good handwriting:

(i) Fairly large movements using finger in a tray of sand or chalk on brown paper for ample muscular, finger and wrist practice; thus:

// \\ = ʍ Ɔ Ɔ CC

(ii) Language psychologists claim that small letters but large in size in script writing should precede capitals. These should be grouped according to their shape.

a b c d e p q o

m n h r f j l i t y u

w v x z k

s

Each stroke should be continuous occupying the space in between the lines. (four-lined books to be used in the beginning), rather than on the line. Letters must be upright, parallel and with equal spacing.

(iii) Spacing of letters is important for neat appearance of writing, but this is difficult for children in forming letters, these should be as close as possible, without touching. At first the rule must be "Letters close, words apart."

(iv) Capital letters must not be taught until all the small letters have been learned. Capitals also can be arranged in groups according to their shape.

Round capitals : O Q C G D

Square Capitals : H N M T Z A X U V M

Half-Square Capitals : E F L K Y I J

Half-Circle Capitals : S P B R

(v) Later, the letters may be joined by giving each small letter a little tailor joiner, but this should not be attempted until the beginning of the 3rd year.

(vi) The teacher should constantly watch the children and help them to sit upright (not slump in the chair). The position of the body, arm, head and paper must be watched carefully. Body should be upright and parallel to the edge of the desk; head to be slightly bent, eyes should be 12" above the papers; edge of the paper should be parallel to the edge of the desk. The hand should rest lightly on the edge of the little finger and side of the wrist.

The pencil should be held lightly in such a way that the first finger can be moved up and down by itself. It should be possible to draw the pencil gently from that child's grip; if that is not possible, the pencil is held with too much strength. Heavy or top light pressure is to be avoided. Modern linguists discourage the use of slates, as the pressure used on slates differs from the pressure used for pencils or pens and hence instils bad habits of writing.

When the pupils have learnt how to write letters, they should practise the writing of words, such as writing their names, standard, name of the school. When writing with flash cards in going on, pupils should practise writing out the sentences from flash-cards. When they have acquired a fair recognition vocabulary they may be introduced to a simple phonic drill, *e.g.* writing words with the same sound *e.g.* and, hand, stand. This will heIp to strengthen the bond between sound and spelling.

Types of Writing Exercises

Writing is a slower process than either spelling or reading. The child's mind can move at its own pace. He has plenty of time to think over what he is doing. As he writes, he thinks about the sentence both as a whole and in its separate parts. For these reasons, the writing exercise has a powerful effect on the child's mind and provides a very good way of fixing vocabulary, spelling and sentence patterns of all kinds. Types, it is not a means of teaching but also a means of fixing what has been learned. Writing can be taught through the following exercises:

(1) ***Transcription:*** To begin with, free composition should be attempted only after the fourth year. The transcription, only sentences already learnt in the reader should be written. Moral sentences should be avoided. Substitution tables can also be used.

(2) ***Dictation:*** This is another exercise for prefocusing handwriting but which should not be introduced to early. It is much more difficult than transcription and should never be given as a test to young beginners. It is a means of fixing and not a testing device. Everything a child writes, must be easy for him.

Dictating when given within limits is a valuable exercise, for the following reasons:

(i) It trains the ear to listen carefully to spoken English sounds and it helps both, listening and speaking.

(ii) It uses the hand as well as the eye for practising the shapes of words and this list far better than oral memorising of spelling.

(iii) It fixes in the pupils mind the divisions of each sentence pattern, because the good teacher, when she dictates, will dictate division-by-division. These divisions are brought to the pupils' notice by sound, appearance and muscular memory.

(iv) Dictation uses the mind's eye. In fact, it is a good preparation for the teacher to put a new word or phrase on the black-board and then after teaching it thoroughly tell the pupils to close their eyes and memorise the looks of it. It is a very effective means of using the visual sense of the child for leading spelling. Another form of writing exercise is the text book exercise of writing sentences and paragraphs.

Kinds of Writing—Script and Cursive

Although for adult writing, running-hand or cursive script is more popular, many countries are now using script writing which is a simplified form of hand-writing. The reason is that script is simpler and easier to learn than cursive, and is better adapted to the child's capacity for motor control. Although the use of script was vigorously opposed at first when an ornate and flowery handwriting was considered beautiful, it has spread in recent years. It is useful specially in the first two years.

Advantages of script writing are:

1. It practically removes the disadvantages of two types of script which the child has to learn to read and write.

2. It is easy to acquire involving only combination of straight lines and circles.

3. It is very legible and forms a base for a permanent style.

4. It improves spelling, as comparison with the printed words is possible and checks mistakes.

5. Dr Ballard, a great advocate of the print script states, from the utilitarian point of view, it is a return to legibility, from the pedagogical point of view it is a return to simplicity and economy of learning and from the prettiness of decoration to beauty of essential structure."

However, even the most ardent advocates of the print script admit that sooner or later, the pupils must switch over to cursive handwriting particularly in the higher classes, where the quantum of written work is much higher. Also the print script is not very fluent. Hence, the cursive style of writing attains the ideal of equipping the student with a style of handwriting that is legible, fast and neat, and a practical style for an adult working life.

Teaching of Composition

Composition is the art of putting our thoughts into words. It is the ultimate aim of all education, and therefore, is perhaps the most important aspect of English teaching and learning in schools. Unfortunately, this is also the only aspect that is most neglected. Due to its great importance, all teaching and learning must lead up to the ability to communicate in English effectively. The days when grammar and composition were taught as separate subjects like science and history are past. Today, grammar and composition form an integral part of the whole English course and they should be taught as such. One of the earliest forms of composition are transcription and dictation. Hence composition is closely related to prose and the reader.

Oral and Written Composition

There are two types of composition—oral and written. Both forms are sadly neglected in our schools. Whatever composition is attempted, is in the form of written composition. But as in the case of other aspects of language teaching such as grammar and reading, so also, composition should be preceded by plenty of oral work.

One of the principal aims of teaching English is acquiring proficiency in speech. The main object is that girls and boys should be able to talk freely. It is only when a student acquires a certain command of the language in speech that he is able to put down something worthwhile on paper. Mr FG French rightly points out that the pupil can give you only what he has within, and no more, and that there is really little distinction between oral and written composition. The main difference is that written composition is slower than oral one. Students will give out their thoughts freely only when they are keenly interested, and want very much to say something.

Aims of Oral Composition

The aims of oral composition are developing the:

(i) ability to describe any given topic.

(ii) ability to converse freely.

(iii) ability to discuss and debate.

(iv) ability to give instructions.

(v) ability to speak a few sentences correctly and continuously on a given topic.

Mr Robert Finch observes that good composition must grow out of a person's own experiences. We write most powerfully when we feel most deeply, and we write convincingly only when we are sincere. Children will not and cannot write good composition unless they have something to say and only when they are interested. Also there should be a desire on their part to want to say it. It is then the teachers business to teach them how to say it well. Once the interest of the child is secured, the rest is comparatively easy.

The earliest oral composition can be based on the children's personal experiences like:

(i) Speaking a few sentences on a known subject.

(ii) Describing a seen picture.

(iii) Describing a person, place or incident.

(iv) Conversing on a topic of interest.

(v) Answering oral questions from a passage already read.

(vi) Listening to a story and retelling it.

During this stage, the teacher should describe, narrate and introduce new words, phrases and sentences side by side. The child listens, observes, drills and assimilates. The topic chosen should be within the range for the child's day to-day experience and not something completely new (*e.g.* Snow covered streets). Thus, selection of topics should be done carefully.

WRITTEN COMPOSITION

After thorough drilling has been done orally, we can proceed to written composition.

Aims of Written Composition

(i) Writing a paragraph correctly.

(ii) Ability to write correct sentences on a certain topic.

(iii) Ability to convey written messages.

(iv) Ability to reply letters.

(v) Simple Essay Writing.

(vi) Writing readable stories.

At the end of the English course, a child should acquire all the above abilities.

Types of Composition

We have to distinguish between controlled and free composition. In controlled composition the students are shown a certain framework within which they must limit themselves. Free composition imposes no such restraint, and the child is left free to give full rein to his ideas and thoughts. In the first three years at least it is advisable to limit the child to controlled composition to avoid a number of discouraging mistakes. Looking to the age and intellectual development of the child, it can be introduced after the fourth year, corresponding to class eight. Early controlled composition can be in the form of transcription, to co-ordinate the muscles of the hand, eye and ear. Every new structure should be practised thoroughly through transcription.

Secondly, answers to the given questions from the reader can be attempted. Substitution tables, rearrangement of sentences matching, joining and completion of sentences, as well as transformation of sentences can be given, based on oral work.

Dictation

Dictation is an important kind of writing exercise for the early stages. It is a means of fixing what is already known. It is a valuable exercise for the following reasons:

(i) It trains the ear to listen carefully to spoken English sound. It helps both listening and speaking.

(ii) It uses the hand as well as the eye for practising the shapes of words.

Such reproduction exercises require plenty of oral preparation. They should be based, as far as possible, on the reader. Guiding points should be left on the board while writing.

Free Composition

Free composition can start from the fourth year corresponding to class nine. The child is forced first to think of ideas. Here again, the importance of oral work must be emphasised. The child is capable of reproducing only what is said by the teacher, or written in the textbook. Teachers do not pay sufficient attention to oral composition in the higher classes. It must be realised that in order to write correct English the pupils must speak good English. When children are trained to attend to their spelling and punctuation, it follows that a good speaker will naturally turn out to be a good writer. The structural approach rightly put great emphasis on oral work. But most teachers look upon composition as only something to be written. They feel that careful correction is only necessary in connection with written work. If they allow careless, bad and slipshod English in oral work, then they cannot expect good written work. The teacher must therefore insist on correct oral English in every English lesson. Children should be encouraged to think before they speak.

Another reason for stereotyped writing of students is the method of dealing with composition in schools. It is a common practice to ask children to write ten sentences on such mundane topics as the cow, crow, dog, school etc. and to accept spiritless writing *e.g.* one essay that came across on "The Dog" ran as follows:

The dog is a small animal. The dog lives in houses. The dog has four legs. The dog has two ears. The dog has one tail. The dog eats meat. The dog loves children. The dog hates cats. The dog loves to play. My dog's name is Moti.

This exercise which has written by a pupil of class six, was awarded full marks. The composition shows no style no method, no aim, no intelligence, and yet there is nothing really grammatical with it.

This is the type of work that is found mostly in our schools. Such writings are no test of one's power of expression or observation. Yet this is the kind of work which is asked for and dished up week after week in most of our schools. In the above exercise in the last sentence the boy stops short where his essay should have really begun when from general he comes to the particular, when he might say something interesting about his dog at home. But the introduction of the teacher and points written on the black-board do not permit these personal observations. Most likely, he mentioned his dog's name because he had nothing else to say in the tenth sentence.

Method of Teaching Composition

Composition exercises should be the genuine expression of genuine perception, which have behind them what the child has experienced, what he has felt or thought, what he has read and studied. Children so have views to express and if adequately encouraged, will come out with some very original performances. In the higher classes, compositions take the form of paragraphs, essays, letter-writing, paraphrasing, translation etc. These should be taught inductively. Specimens or models should be displayed which should be discussed, studied etc. The qualities of a good paragraph or essay should be elicited from the pupils. They should practise what they learn from the black-board models.

In essay writing the first stage should be the construction of the paragraph, and the aim should be to teach the principles of paragraph structure. Pupils must practise the formation of sentences that go to make up the paragraph. In the higher classes, more attention should be paid to continuous oral composition. This is the best preparation for continuous written composition. Single sentence answers are necessary but at the end of each stage in a composition discussion, the pupil should be made to give orally in continuous sentences what has been discussed up to that point. The same holds true of reading lessons too. Whenever the teacher finds that the written composition is not satisfactory he should resort to oral composition as a corrective, because it is an accepted principle that he who speaks well will write well too.

Thus the main purpose of teaching composition is to enable the pupil to express himself clearly and accurately, to see things for himself and to describe them composition writing should train his imagination and broaden his sympathies, increase his powers of thinking and reasoning, so that eventually he develops a feeling for language, a love for and appreciation of good literature.

Positive Approach to Correction Work

The most important point to remember while correcting the pupils exercises is that corrections must not prove to the pupil that he is utterly useless; but must be source of encouragement. Corrections must aim at developing the creative impulse in the child and must stimulate the child to improvement. When certain mistakes are pointed out, the teacher must make it a point at the same time to ring to the child's notice where he has succeeded. His efforts at good work and improvement must be appreciated. This will make him realise that mistakes spoil good work and it will also create an attitude of welcome rather that criticism of the teacher's criticism. Thus, the approach of the teacher must be both positive and negative, and not negative alone.

The purpose of correcting compositions and other homework is fourfold:

(i) To judge whether the matter is complete and suitable.

(ii) To discover and correct mistakes.

(iii) To check whether the pupils are able to arrange their ideas and express them clearly.

(iv) To inform pupils as to how he compares with the standard expected of him.

Method of Correcting Composition

To diminish her own work and arrive at maximum improvement every teacher must devise her own plan of correction. Many teachers have evolved a language of symbols, *e.g.,* sp. for spelling mistake when the child is too imaginative? When the matter is not appropriate, when the grammar is incorrect and so on. Some teachers believe in the exchange of books in the classroom for correction. The main point is that children must be conversant with these symbols and know exactly where they have erred.

A well-devised plan of correction is very necessary. The teacher must not correct too many errors at the same time, e g. in the early stages the teacher should concentrate on spelling, punctuation use of capitals legible writing and so on and not worry about minor errors as meet use of adjectives or Metaphors. Similarly in the later stages he should attach more importance to fluency, clearness of expression and sense of construction rather than to correct spellings or construction. As Hartog puts it. "He should criticize not the bricks but the architecture."

However what the teacher corrects in a particular lesson will depend more on what the teacher has taught. Large scale marking in red and blue will only discourage pupils but piecemeal correction helps to focus the attention on glaring errors. Very often the teacher should merely underline the mistakes and allow the pupil to correct himself. If he cannot do this, the mistake is not a slip but imperfect knowledge. In that case correction should take the form of more drill-work, to fill the gaps of knowledge that may have occurred in his teaching.

The usefulness of correction, work can be increased if the teacher makes a list of mistakes common to most pupils in each homework. These can be discussed in class, thus removing any misunderstanding or doubts in the minds of students. Such a discussion is always more productive than laborious markings in the books.

Discussion Method

This leads us to the discussion method of correcting homework. It is a Hartog 'method' described by Ballard in "Teaching and Testing English". The teacher reads one of the essays and then the author of it is asked to criticize it. He is welcome to decide whether he has achieved the object in view or not after he has had his say, the class is invited to participate in the discussion. But the ultimate judge of his success or failure is the author himself based upon the views of the teacher and his friends.

A discussion of three or four essays on these lines generally covers the faults and merits of the essays of nearly the whole class. Every pupil gets a turn. Ballard claims that this method develops both the creative and the critical faculties of the students. Pupils are encouraged to find merits as well as faults. Morever when corrected homework is returned mistakes as well as teacher's remarks must be discussed. The discussion helps to drive home the points the teacher wishes to make. In this manner, homework can be a means of teaching as well as testing. When it serves the purpose of testing only, the usefulness is greatly reduced.

A teacher must bear in mind the following points while correcting composition:

(i) Corrections should make him pay attention to all the mistakes and give drills for practice.

(ii) Corrections should never discourage the pupil.

(iii) Corrections should be a stepping-stone to the improvement of composition work.

(iv) Teachers should show the pupil that they have read his work with interest, and should appreciate and criticize constructively.

❐

13

Teaching of Literature and Prose

Teaching literature helps in developing cognitive and affective aspects of the students and provides the awareness and understanding of cultural and social development. Sometime literature contributes in revolutionising the national life, because there is force in words to motivate or encourage people for active participation in national movements. The literature helps in understanding the present on the basis of past and provides a guideline for future action. The nature of literature is philosophical as well as historical. A literature in real sense preserves the culture, values and lifestyle of a society which is transmitted to new generation. If a literature of social is destroyed it means that its cultures, values and real lifestyle are also destroyed. Nalanda and Taxshila libraries were destroyed to destroy our vedic culutre. The literature is the major source of enjoyment. Teaching a literature relates the present to past tradition, conduct, culture, beliefs, values and mental tendency. A literature generates higher and liberal thoughts in the minds of the students. It also encourages and guides for future development. It develops the philosophy of life and provides the awareness about man's nature.

Objectives of Teaching Literature

The literature is available in various forms. Prose, poems, stories, biographies, dramas, novels, autobiographies. The review of the forms reveals the teaching objectives of literature. Some general objectives of teaching literature have been summarised.

BS Bloom taxonomy of teaching objectives provides the general format into three domains.

(1) Cognitive domain, (2) Affective domain and (3) Conative or psychomotor domain. These domains are classified into six categories which are also used for classifying teaching objectives.

The objectives of teaching literature are cognitive and affective. The cognitive objectives are knowledge, understanding, creative or critical analysis. The affective objectives are, feelings, values, appreciation, beliefs and attitudes and feeling of emotional integration or patriotism.

PRINCIPLES OF TEACHING LITERATURE

The following are the main principles of teaching literature.

1. ***Interest of Teacher in Teaching Language and Literature:*** This principle of interest in teaching is very significant. The teachers involvement in reading English literature and teaching literature depend on his interest. The involvement in teaching encourages students for the participation in classroom teaching and also develops the interest.

2. ***Availability of Higher and Good Literature in the Library:*** The library of an educational institute should have the higher and rich literature, so that teachers and students can go through it and enjoy the higher literature. This may raise level of thinking and standard of teachers.

3. ***Various Types of Literature should be Included in the Books:*** At school level, it is essential that all forms of literature should be included in the text books. But at higher level there should be separate books on each form of the literature. This type of provision may provide the

awareness about the various forms of the literature. A teacher should know the objectives and methods of teaching of these forms of the literature. During his teaching, he should emphasise the sensitive spots to involve the emotions of the students.

4. ***Literary and Cultural Programmes of Literature should be Organised in Schools and Colleges:*** On the various occassions literary and cultural programmes should be organised and experts and eminent scholars should be invited for guest lectures, so that the students may get the opportunities for the interaction. The students should also be given opportunities in debates, group discussion and seminars, etc. There should be a competition on essay writing, or any other form of literature to encourage students for developing language competency.

5. ***A Teacher should Encourage his Students Write any Form of Literature:*** The teacher should have the two main focus of teaching literature.

   (1) To enable students for literary realisations.

   (2) To enable students for writing these on the various forms of the literature.

   The students should be encouraged for easy and simple writing and gradually, they should proceed to difficult and complex theme. The students works should be encouraged and praised in class to raise their level of aspiration.

TECHNIQUES OF TEACHING ENGLISH LITERATURE

Teaching method involves various techniques of teaching for employing it effectively. There are several techniques of teaching which are used according to the need and requirement of classroom presentation. The following are the main techniques of teaching English literature:

1. ***Question-Answer Technique:*** Some techniques of teaching are also classified as method of teaching. It depends on the use in classroom teaching. If a teacher is presenting his topic by using lecture method and makes use of question-answer for some teaching points, then question answer is used as technique or vice-versa. In question-answer method, teacher uses lecture for explaining some concepts, lecture is used technique of teaching.

2. ***Explanation Technique:*** This technique is used for explaining some concepts, theories, principles and laws in detail to make it clear to the students. The components of these aspects of content are analysed thoroughly to provide full or true understanding of the concepts. While description technique is used for teaching facts and events logically or in chronological order. The different concepts are presented by the use of this technique to make teaching effective and understandable. The technique requires mastery of the language which he employs in classroom verbal interaction as well as mastery of the content. The nature of such content is abstract and the teacher tries to make it concrete by employing explanation technique. The teacher has to locate the need of the students and where they feel the need for explanation.

3. ***Exposition Technique:*** The exposition technique is used in detail in the sequence of presentation of the content for providing the understanding of the content. The narration technique is the suplementary or supporting device of exposition because it is always in brief. The narration technique is used for new facts and concepts while exposition technique is used for dealing the whole unit of teaching in detail from beginning to its end. The exposition

is very specific. For example, if the concept of learning is taught, the description technique provides its meaning, definition, nature and its theories and laws in detail, but language learning is taught by using exposition technique, because it requires knowledge of verbal learning.

4. ***Narration Technique*** or statement technique is used by the teacher along with illustration, teaching aids and after question. In developing question the narration technique is very helpful for the teacher to highlight the new concept which the teacher intends to convey to his students. It is considered an important and useful technique for teaching English literature.

5. ***Illustration Technique:*** This technique is for developing thinking ability as well as imagination of the students. This technique is supported by the maxim of teaching abstract to concrete. This technique reduces the complexity of the content and enables the students to understand easily. It makes presentation interesting and effective. The illustration should be related to the real life situations of the students and meaningful to them. Two types of illustrations are used in English teaching verbal illustration and visual illustration. Sometime visual illustrations are very effective because it involves two senses-audio and visual. These illustrations should be used at the appropriate stage of teaching in classroom. It is supported by maxims of teaching.

6. ***Supervised Study Technique:*** This technique is used after presentation of the content. It is used at the assimilation stage. The students have to practice or study according to their pace in class or in the library. The students remain active and teacher has to supervise students activities of learning individually where they require the help or want clarification of the content. It is used in

both the situations in classroom interaction and also for remedial teaching it develops the mastery of the subject matter. It is different from earlier techniques of English teaching.

Characteristics of an Effective English Teacher

It is said that effective teachers are born. They cannot be made effective through teacher training. Now educationists and psychologists have proved that effective teachers can be produced or prepared through training. It is the basic assumption of this statement that teacher behaviour is modifiable Teaching skills, competencies are developed by using the feedback devices micro-teaching, verbal-interaction technique, simulated training and T-group training etc.

According to Rabindra Nath Tagore, "A teacher is like a burning lamp. A burning lamp can light another lamp if it burns own flame."

The students are like lamps which are not burning their flames, though possess the basic requirements or potentialities. A teacher is like burning lamp who can light other (students) lamps to burn their own flame.

It is common saying that teacher's qualities can be stated as John Latin. Here John means student and Latin means content. An effective teacher must know student as well as mastery of his content.

The teacher's characteristics have been enumerate in terms of teacher's roles. An effective teacher plays his three roles effectively—Philosopher, Guide and Friend. Here the philosopher indicates the mastery of the subject. The guide means to help the students in their learning difficulties and provides remediation. A Friend means that teacher must have good rapport with the students to know their problems and have "the sympathy to raise their level of aspiration for higher attainment of life.

The following characteristics are essential for an effective English teacher:

(1) He should have the knowledge and skills of English language: reading, writing, speaking and listening.

(2) He should know the purpose of teaching English as first language and as second language English teaching.

(3) He should have the understanding of various forms of literature—prose, poetry, stories, drama and novels.

(4) He should have the interest and "favourable attitude towards English teaching as well as content.

(5) He should be able to identify the objectives of teaching of various forms of literature and able to write it in behavioural terms.

(6) He should have the awareness and practice of teaching methods, techniques, devices and maxims of teaching.

(7) He should be able to diagnose the learning difficulties of teaching English and prepare remedial instructions for those concepts.

(8) He should be able to differentiate between language teaching and English literature teaching at various stages.

(9) He should possess high moral character because he is the leader of the students, to guide them for the right path. The students generally follow and imitate his teacher.

(10) He should have the devotion in teaching profession and also punctual of his duties.

(11) An effective teacher uses however to avoid monotony of the class climate. He makes the classroom climate alive and receptive.

(12) He should be impartial in his behaviour. He should be above all cast, community religion etc.

He should attain the mastery of teaching skills and also the mastery of his subject matter. He should come into the class with full preparation. There should be close relation between the saying and doing aspect. Though the doing aspect of a teacher is more effective than preaching or saying aspect. He should be ideal or model to his students. An effective teacher always enjoys or seeks pleasure through his teaching and has great involvement in his teaching. An English teacher should have expertise in his teaching language as well as literature. A English literature teacher is a philosopher as well as artist in his presentation.

Procedure of Teaching English Literature

Before entrining to the classroom, a teacher should prepare his teaching lesson of English literature. The following steps are followed for developing instruction procedure of English literature:

1. Selection of teaching topic from any form of literature—prose, poetry, story, drama and novel.
2. The topic is analysed into its components and these components are further divided into elements or teaching points which are arranged a learning sequence.
3. The previous knowledge required for dealing with the topic, is also identified.
4. Teaching objectives are identified in terms of Bloom's category and these objectives are written in behavioural terms.
5. Presentation of topic or teaching at interactive stage be planned into four aspects.
   (a) Teaching points;
   (b) Teacher's activities;
   (c) Students activities;
   (d) Evaluation of objectives;

Teaching points of instruction procedure are classified as follow:

(1) Introducing topic to the students with the help of introducing questions.

(2) Model reading is done by the teacher

(3) A teacher has to state the topic of teaching

(4) The model reading is followed by imitation reading on the students.

(5) A teacher has to select some difficult words of the passage or stanza to write its meaning in Hindi on blackboard. The students have to copy down from the blackboard.

(6) A teacher has to organize pronuncial drill for the correct pronunciation of some difficult words.

(7) A teacher has to ask some recaptulatory questions to assess, whether the student could follow or not. The teacher will try to remove the learning difficulty of the students.

(8) At the end the teacher will assigns some home work for the practice or self-study. The stage of teaching is known as post-active stage.

(9) A teacher has to ask the students for silent reading without moving their lips and without producing any sound.

(10) A teacher has to ask some comprehension questions or developing questions. The students will try to respond.

The teacher has to write the blackboard summary. The words which are used for pronunciation questions, drill and meanings are noted down. The developing responses are also written on the blackboard. At the end home work should be noted down on the blackboard. The above steps are used for designing a teaching lesson plan for teaching practice.

TEACHING THE READING OF PROSE

"Some books are to be tasted, others to be swallowed and some few to be chewed and digested."

This famous dictum of Francis Bacon holds good to this day, and gives us valuable guidance on the developing of right reading habits in children. All schools have different types of text books of readers prescribed to encourage children to read as much as possible. The three types of readers all encourage reading—they differ only in their immediate goal.

Intensive Reading

In dealing with the Intensive Reader in schools, the pupil is required not only to learn to comprehend the lessons, but must learn to master the structures and vocabulary. A person who learns English as a foreign language, is expected to surpass even the native speaker in the mastery over the written language. This can be achieved through intensive reading. Hence intensive reading forms a very important aspect of learning a foreign language. In fact, experts like Dr West regard intensive reading as the most important activity of foreign language learning.

Jesperson Claims, "The main point is for the pupils to be occupied with the text repeatedly in such a way that they do not lose sight of the meaning, so that they may thus become so familiar with it that they know it almost or entirely by heart without having been directly required to commit it to memory."

The language of the intensive reader should pass into the pupils working vocabulary so that he should be able to actually use the words he learns therein. The intensive reader should be based on the structural syllabus, containing interesting and well-graded reading material accompanied by colourful pictures to create an interest in the lesson. All reading lessons should be preceded by plenty of oral discussions, in which difficult words, phrases and ideas should be clearly explained by the teacher. Lessons based on the intensive reader should have provision for both reading aloud and silent reading, to give the greatest benefits to a learner of English.

Extensive Reading

The main aim of extensive reading is to create an interest in reading for pleasure. Extensive reading should encourage the pupils to visualise what is read so as to make reading of prose a living experience. The primary objective of this reading is comprehension and not detailed language study. Also, since the intensive reader is based on structures, it tends to present a stilted and unidiomatic picture of the language. To get a feel of the real language without the rigid constraints of the structures, the child should be encouraged to read as much as possible. Detailed attention to meaning of new words and phrases is hence discouraged. The pupil is expected to understand the meaning of words when presented in their proper context. In this manner, extensive reading adds to the recognition vocabulary of the pupils, and creates an interest in reading good literature.

Wherever new words occur in an extensive reader, which is popularly called a "rapid reader" in schools, children should be encouraged to make use of the dictionary or "Thesarus" to find out the meanings. A broad drift of the passage should by explained by the teacher, particularly the use of idioms and other ornamentation of the language. The learners should also be guided to discover the main sentence of the paragraphs, so as to enable them to acquire adult reading habits where the amount of matter read is enormous. Such identification of the main idea of the paragraph is also a useful exercise for helping comprehension. The main difference between intensive and extensive reading may be summed up in the following words:

"In intensive reading, a child learns to read, in extensive reading, a child practises what he has learnt."

Broad questions, testing comprehension are generally planned language exercises for extensive reading material.

Supplementary Reading

No teacher of English is satisfied with the amount of reading that children do in class, whether it is intensive or extensive. Some amount of subsidiary reading is a must for students of English. Supplementary reading however must not be confused with library reading. Supplementary reading is done and tested in set lessons, and constitutes supervised reading as compared to library reading which is neither directed-nor supervised. The supplementary reader should preferably be of standard at least as simple as the reader used for the class, or lone standard lower than the pupils class. The structures and vocabulary learned in the reader should be practised in the supplementary readers. At least one period a week should be set aside for supplementary reading. The main activity during such periods should be silent reading of the prescribed passages. Before the silent reading, the teacher should provide a few broad questions to provide a goal and direction to the reading. After the reading the passage should be discussed to discover how much the pupils have understood.

A good scheme to encourage supplementary reading in class is to have many copies of two different books of similar difficulty and interest level. Let half the class take home one set and the other half the second half for reading. During the next week, the books are given to the other half of the class. After all the children have gone through both the books, they are given an opportunity in class to question each other. This activity can be turned into a game if the class is divided on basis of houses of girls versus boys. In this manner, reading and discussion of two books can be done every month. One point to bear in mind while selecting books for such supplementary reading exercises is that the books selected for reading should be fairly easy, preferably of a standard lower than the one for which they are prescribed. This encourages spontaneous reading in children and provides a tremendous sense of achievement and satisfaction. This is also a great impetus to reading on their own.

TYPES OF READING

Reading Aloud

There is always a good deal of reading aloud or Oral Reading carried on when teaching English. But, in actual practice very little real reading is done, because a major portion of what goes under the name of reading aloud is what Dr Ballard calls "barking at print". Whatever reading is done is ruined by indistinct pronunciation and "eating up of words". Part of the difficulty is because English is a foreign language. But the main difficulty lies in the fact that pupils are not taught to read aloud properly in their mother-tongue. If they, cannot read with expression in their mother-tongue, how can they do so in English?

Objectives of Reading Aloud

The teaching of reading aloud has three main objectives:

1. We may wish to give practice in pronunciation, articulation, correct intonation, right emphasis, tone, speed, etc., using reading as a stage towards learning to speak English well.

2. We may wish to test the pupil's knowledge of English words and phrases, and whether he knows how to pronounce them, how to phrase words, how to enunciate clearly.

3. We may wish to develop reading as an art, so that pupils may learn to read aloud, with proper expression and may learn, through their reading, to convey the feeling behind the words to their listeners.

The main aim is making pupils realise the importance of making every word and syllable distinctly heard and understood by all so that it makes intelligible the meaning and significance of the general drift of the passage read.

In reading aloud, posture and speed are both important, and due attention should be paid to these. Teachers should read first as a model and not as mere routine, while pupils should read much later after the passage is understood. Speed is not necessary let the student take his time and not attempt wild guesses in the interest of speed. Reading aloud is essential at the end of a lesson when expression can be given to meaning. Reading aloud can be greatly helped by dramatic work and good recitation work, as many students take part in playlets where each student should be taught to read in a natural manner.

Chorus reading should be discouraged as a rule. It may be done occasionally in lower classes to add a little variety to the lesson, or to give these children who are diffident and shy a chance to let themselves go. But it is not a good practice from the teaching point of view because poorer readers tend to take shelter behind the noise made by the good ones. Language experts like EW Manzel believe that the best results related to reading can be obtained through oral reading methods. Oral reading provides the wrong setting for the teaching of reading for pleasure and profit, for the following reasons:

Firstly, it deters the reader—he does not want to be conspicuous.

Secondly, other people seldom want to hear him. Moreover oral reading is far less efficient than silent reading for private use. A habitual reader cannot be an extensive reader, nor a fast one, nor an efficient one with respect of understanding of what he reads. The attention paid to uttering the sounds and listening to them is a distinct obstruction to understanding.

However, with all these limitations reading aloud has its place in teaching of English. Great literature, prose and especially poetry, cannot be appreciated unless read aloud, for they call for utterances. Moreover, oral reading trains the pupil to express himself properly in spoken English and reading helps the hearers in understanding the passage read. The emotional impact of poetry is also best conveyed when read aloud with feeling, hence reading aloud has a definite place in the teaching of poetry.

Silent Reading

Reading aloud is not the best training or preparation for thinking and assimilating the subject matter. It is just like parrot reading, where pupils concentrate on the pronouncing of words rather than on thought content. Adequate attention can be given to thought only when one is not required to read it aloud. It follows then that reading for thought should be silent reading. Thus for most people, silent reading is more important than oral reading. Training in silent reading is hence must important for most of our pupils and it is to this that the teacher of English has to devote a great deal of attention.

Oral reading will lead to silent reading. The aims of silent reading are pleasure and profit, to be able to read for interest and to get information. The advantages of silent reading are that it is quicker, and hence saves time, it enables attention and energy to be concentrated on meaning and so saves division of attention. This results in greater assimilation of information.

Improving Silent Reading

To read well silently requires as much training as oral reading. Teachers must explain that silent reading is not whispering or murmuing words, but reading with the mind's eye. We cannot expect ability for silent reading to develop in the early stages of teaching English. Until pupils have a fair recognition vocabulary and know the pronunciation of a fairly large number of words, they will not benefit much from silent reading. But a beginning can be made in the second year with easy stories which should then be tested with questions.

In order to improve silent reading the teachers must know the mechanics of reading silent reading the eye does not proceed steadily along the line of print, but stops from time to time, possibly four or five times in a time. Then there is a rapid movement from the end of one line to the beginning of the next. During the movement of the eyes, there is no perception. We read only during the pauses when the eyes are not moving. To gain speed, it is necessary to reduce the number of pauses, or increase the number of words recognised in a single pause.

Thus silent reading can be improved in three ways:

1. Developing perception of a number of words in a single pause.
2. Steadying eye movement to a regular rhythm.
3. Improving speed without effecting comprehension.

Vocabulary difficulties should be reduced so that attention can be paid to form of words. There should not be more than 3 or 4 new, words per page.

Dr West who was one of the greatest advocates of silent reading for Indian students mentions these four points for teaching reading:

1. The pupil should derive pleasure and a sense of power from the very beginning.
2. Words should be learnt by practice in reading situations and not memorized as vocabulary.
3. New words should appear at regular intervals, and not on mass.
4. Reading matter should be suited to the age of the pupil. Aimless silent reading should be avoided. The teacher should always give a couple of simple questions to the students to provide direction to their reading activity.

❐

14

Teaching of Poetry and Other Activities

Unfortunately, the matter and method of teaching poetry to Indian students do not conform with this aim. Most of the English poetry taught in our secondary schools should not be there at all such as poems with obscurity of language difficulty in thought and sentiments or association of ideas. Many of these are unsuitable for Indian children. Although many of these poems contain thought of great poetic value, yet they may be totally unsuitable for children. Again in a single stanza, there may be too many unknown words which need elaborate explanations. Unless a poem is fully understood, it cannot be enjoyed. The success of a poetry lesson in Indian schools will depend on what poems are chosen. Children like repetitions, refrains, and rhymes. Rhyme introduces into poetry not only magic and charm, but also actual melody. Poems for young children should abound in rhymes and refrains. Children also love stories. Tales should be short and direct in their appeal. Childhood is a period of freedom and fantasy. This stage should not be burdened with moral sayings, or about the glories of man. These are out of tune with a child's merry spirit. Simple things like rivers, mountains, ships, caves, flowers etc. fascinate children. These are subjects dear to the child's heart.

Thus, according to Ryburn in order to give pleasure poetry must not be designed as an examination subject in the curriculum.

Nothing destroys the beauty of a piece of writing more effectively than have it prescribed as an examination subject. The aim of teaching poetry in schools must not be utilitarian—but to give pleasure and provide variety in the intensive study of the Reader. This giving of pleasure is the surest way to establish a foundation for appreciation which will develop later. Real appreciation of English poetry is not the work of the school. That is the task of University education. It has rightly been pointed out that if prose is compared to walking (moving), poetry may be compared to dancing (rising, above the earth's surface). But generally, in life prose is enjoyed more than poetry. The reason is that we are exposed more to prose than poetry.

Aim of Teaching Poetry

The purpose of poetry teaching in the curriculum is to develop the aesthetic sense of the pupils, and appreciation of the beautiful. Appreciation of beauty is essential to change the ugly scenes in life. One of the most abiding arts that education can impart to children is to develop their sense of beauty, and this is a great responsibility of the teacher. In order to instill this love, the teacher must be a lover of beauty himself.

Appreciation of poetry is an experience. It is not primarily critical but creative. When a poet writes a poem he carefully selects the words, rhymes and sounds. The reader creates anew this poem for himself. It is the teacher's business to arouse interest and the children's awareness to this living experience. Poetry is Beauty—beauty of form, language, thoughts, moods and feelings. It is upto the teacher to bring to the child's awareness and insight into this beauty. There should be a lightening of the emotions, and appreciation of the beautiful.

Poetry can be caught, it cannot be taught. A poem that is dead to the teacher will appear dead to the student as well. For a being emotion the teacher must make it live. What matters is the zest and fire of life, enthusiasm and freshness.

It is therefore, best for the students if the teacher avoids teaching any poem she herself does not particularly like. Do not spoil the beauty of a poem with personal prejudices. The study of English today no longer enjoys the position it did 50 years ago. Today, the teaching of poetry is not done with the purpose of bringing to the children's notice the vast treasures of the English language. It must be taught for enjoyment of thought, feeling, imagery and rhythm. It should never be used as a drill in the teaching of language. There should not be detailed exercises in a poetry lesson as we have for prose. Tho children should feel from the beginning that the poetry lesson is different from other lessons.

The teacher should try to read, listen to and enjoy good poetry himself. It is difficult to arouse enthusiasm in others if you have no enthusiasm yourself. The emotion aroused by poetry can be transferred from the teacher to pupil in fact, if this does not take place in the beginning itself, there is no hope of the pupils acquiring a feeling for it. Appreciation of literature is a matter of enthusiasm, of feeling strongly. If this is found in the teacher it will be transferred automatically to the pupil.

Method of Teaching Poetry

Literature cannot be treated in a set manner. Poetry is an expression of emotion—a thing of spirit and enthusiasm. The teacher should follow the device he thinks best will arouse interest and enjoyment of the pupils. Many pitfalls can be avoided in the teaching of poetry with sincere effect.

Avoid spoiling the unity of the poem by lengthy explanations of words and phrases. If you think one of two words needs explanation do this before you begin reciting or reading the poem. Another way is to read the poem as a whole and give explanations afterwards as they are out of the children's own comments. On the, whole teacher should not explain too much. Remember that the meaning is often made clear through context. Poetry is not a matter for examination but for delight. It is true that complete appreciation is helped by good understanding, but it is not necessary for that understanding to be put into words, especially the words of young children or beginners. We like the colours in a picture, the lift of a tune, the taste of a piece of chocolate, but we would not be able to put that appreciation into words. Music words and rhythm have attractions which need not be described. As long as the essentials are made clear let the poem speak for itself through its own musk and rhyme.

Never allow pupils to repeat the poem line by line after the teacher. This old-fashioned method kills and stifles all appreciation. Very often, the young children may join in the recitation of a rhyme jungle with the teacher. Group work and chorus work can be done lower classes to provide variety and avoid monotony; but generally speaking, such occasions should be few. Chorus recitation encourages slovenly habits of speech as individual faults cannot be corrected.

Importance of Teacher's Recitation

All this leads us to the ultimate conclusion that for a poetry lesson to be a success, the teacher must be a flawless reader of English. Reciting the poem well is half the battle won. Reading poetry well is worth more than all the explanations, meanings and paraphrasing that can be given. Poetry belongs first to speech and only secondarily to print. For a teacher to put across to his class the complete message of a poem so that the students are entranced, the essential qualities are sympathy between him and the audience, an intelligent grasp of the message realisation of the mood of the poem and a pleasing and audible voice. The pitch of the voice is also important. If it is too high or harsh or cannot adjust itself to the size of the room, it is bound to detract from the interest of the reading. If it lacks naturalness and simplicity, it will produce a forced effect. Failure to do justice to the mood of the poem or failure to appreciate properly its rhythm is a serious drawback. Thus, how much the message and beauty of it will be conveyed to the student will depend on how well the teacher recites it. To read it well all one has to do is respond to its rhythm which is engendered by emotion and not by metrical rules. If the teacher is not moved by the emotion of a poem, he cannot teach it. If he has been moved, he will feel the emotion and then read the lines, in the natural intonation of speech, he will enter into its spirit, and the spirit of and mood of the poet. He will not only catch the rhythm easily, but something of the inspiration of the poet himself. The inspired teacher will make the poet speak again through him, and children will share his enjoyment of the poem.

The teacher must use his imagination in his approach to the poem and find some way of introducing it which will appeal to the children and will link up with something they have experienced before. Treat your poetry period as an intimate time when you have your children gathered around you in an informal group in which your enthusiasm can be easily caught. Thus, they will look forward to the period when you take them into a new world of rhythm and rhyme, leading them ultimately to an appreciation of Literature.

METHODS OF INTRODUCING POEMS

(1) **Biographical Method:** In this method introduction is done by introducing the poet and his life story. This method is appropriate when children know something about the poet and are interested in the poem. This becomes a very long introduction. Preferably the biographical approach should be done only after the poem is taught in high classes.

(2) **Explanatory Method:** In this method, the poem is introduced by giving the gist of the poem in the beginning. It is not a very good method of introduction.

Defects: Writing difficult words out of context on the black-board makes them more difficult. Haddow claims that if a poem is read well the children are bound to catch the spirit of the poem and they will understand the poem themselves. Word-by-word dissection is not required. If the teacher himself, cannot understand the poem at the second and third readings, how can we expect the children to understand it? Jotting of difficult words on the blackboard may be done in higher classes. Giving the outline of the poem is necessary only in the case of defected poems or in higher classes. A better method is to allow the children to catch the spirit of the poem themselves.

(3) **Synthetic Method of Teaching Poetry:** According to this method of teaching the teacher draws the whole poem from the children by skilful questioning which involves an active participation of the pupils. The teacher must read the poem as a model, while children listen and try to catch the rhythm and spirit of the poem. Alexander Haddow states that there is not set method for teaching poetry. Poetry is beauty and beauty is truth. Teaching poetry is like making love; there are no set rules—each individual has his own way of doing it. To be a successful teacher all you need is love of poetry and then the method is your own. The most important thing is to make children feel and not know, to make children love the beautiful and to deepen that love through understanding. That is the only and best method. But teaching poetry is like life that must have certain principles. These will vary with the class and children.

Commenting on the ideal method of teaching poetry Haddow states, *"Read each poem twice, give the children time to form their own impressions, invite them to criticise and help them in doing so. Let the poetry period be, as far as possible, a period of joy, a period of pondering over things they love already. Let them choose for themselves the poems they are to learn by heart, each choosing his own favourites. Thus only can we develop a taste for poetry and train their ear to the variety of beautiful sounds. Thus only can we rouse in them some idea of the wealth of poetry that lies before them. Remember that we must aim at turning out readers of poetry, not students of poetry."*

Memorisation of Poems

Modern opinion is in favour of recitation but there should be no compulsion about memorising poems. If children enjoy and read a poem constantly, they will learn it by heart without realising it. Competitions and recitation games can be organised to encourage this. Children's enjoyment and appreciation of poems increase when they are required to memorise and recite them. We must remember that originally poetry was meant to be recited and sung and not read.

Poems selected for recitation should be really enjoyable and should have rhythm. Children love strong beats. A poem should be committed to memory only after it is thoroughly understood. Poem memorised in this manner are later used by children to express their own sentiment in the right context.

To encourage children to select and memorise poems that appeal to them, there must be a separate anthology of poems prescribed for each class instead of having poems interspersed with prose lessons in the reader. The prescribed poems should be easy to understand to ensure maximum enjoyment. Poems about Indian life and Indian scenes are desirable for teaching poetry to Indian children.

Elocution competitions, dramatic and recitation matches all encourage memorisation of good poems. Detailed questions on poems dealt in the class should be avoided, as such bookish treatment mars the beauty of poetry.

CO-CURRICULAR AND NON-FORMAL ACTIVITIES IN LANGUAGE LEARNING

(1) **The Spoken Aspect:** Group singing, prayers, debates, elocutions and dramatisation:

Language is, primarily meant to be a means of communication, and hence the spoken form is always more important than the written form. As far as the function of English is concerned as an important language of communication and a link language, its place in the national set-up of the country cannot be over-emphasised. Moreover, English is a foreign language and not known very well by a large majority of Indians hence extra attention must be paid by every school in instilling correct habits of pronunciation in the students.

Good pronunciation is the hall-mark of culture and therefore, every teacher must take pains to imbibe good pronunciation in the children. The normal school-day syllabus provides very scanty opportunities for the children to learn to practice good pronunciation. Moreover the manner and method in which English is taught in India gives rise to very faulty pronunciation. The regional influence also mars good pronunciation. It is therefore, essential that a concentrated effort to instill good pronunciation in our pupils be undertaken.

In teaching prose and poetry, a teacher of English should pay minute attention to the pronunciation of the pupils. For this, it is an undoubted fact that the pronunciation of the teacher himself must be flawless and above blame. However, no amount of curricular work is enough to provide enough practice and drill work essential for this. Hence, due attention should be paid to these co-curricular activities in the school which provide the students with opportunities to improve their pronunciations.

The teacher herself must have a sound knowledge of English phonetics and how the different English sounds are produced. She should also be aware that the spoken English language differs from other native languages in three main areas: Intonation, stress and rhythm.

Stress—Weak and Strong: Important words have a strong stress *e.g.,* nouns, adjectives, principal verbs and adverbs. Stress changes the meaning completely *e.g.,* in the sentence "Don't you give it to anybody the meaning changes dramatically when the stress is shifted to each word.

Rhythm: Rhythm means stress at regular intervals. According to Daniel Jones, people speak about 300 syllables per minute or 5 syllables per second.

The following activities can help to instill better pronunciation in pupils:

Group Singing and Prayer: Singing of group songs and prayer meetings where opportunities for group singing are provided is a very good exercise for practice in intonation, stress and rhythm. Music has a universal appeal for children, and even a normally shy and introverted child will open up and join gustily in group singing at the slightest provocation. Group singing is especially useful for such shy children who tend to hide behind the noise made by the class. Again, it is a well accepted fact that memorisation becomes much easier for poetry and music than it is for prose. Hence, group singing can provide a pleasurable drill activity for the formation and strengthening of correct pronunciation exercises for children. A prayer meeting has the additional advantage of appealing to the children's religious sentiments. Singing in chorus has thus a very beneficial effect on pronunciation and children acquire the right intonation and rhythm without being aware of it being a necessary drill. All this makes speech training a really pleasurable activity. The most important point to bear in mind at all times is that the teacher should adopt a friendly and sympathetic attitude towards the children. At no time should a child's pronunciation be made fun of ever, and the child should never be made to feel self-conscious of his speech habits.

Debates and Elocutions: These activities provide excellent opportunities for correction of pronunciation and speech training. Traditionally, good poetry was meant to be recited and heard, and the true value of poetry is in bearing it being well recited. Elocutions and prizes or awards instituted for debating provide children with a very strong motivation to participate in these activities. If the children are permitted to choose the poems of their choice, this will add to their zest for reciting them with proper expression and emotion. When a child knows that he is taking part in a competition and that he is going to recite before an audience, he will put an extra effort in his preparation and this has a tremendous advantage over normal daily school exercises in reading.

Debates have the added advantage of providing the students with opportunities for organizing their thoughts and ideas, and presenting them in a logical and systematic manner. Thus, apart from giving the children good practice in public speaking, debates train the children to collect information from different sources, organise the material and present it in a coherent and logical manner. When debates are organised as inter-house or inter-school activities, children learn to work and operate as a team.

Dramatisation: Children have a natural bent for dramatic invention and activity and this has a universal appeal for them. In their flair for drama, children put in everything that they have seen and experienced and this makes dramatisation a treasure house of practice in forming good speech habits in children. The educational possibilities of dramatisation for a teacher of English are limitless, and this is further proved by the vast variety of small plays and one-act plays available in English. Thus dramatisation is a very useful teaching device for language teachers interested in improving the pronunciation of the students and inculcating correct speech habits. Dramatisation has the added advantage of harnessing speech and oral expression to facial expression, gesture and movement or action. It is thus, a means of communication between the actors and the audience. Dramatisation can be either incidental and spontaneous in the classroom where a piece from prose and poetry may be dramatised by the children on the spot of the moment, or it may be formally presented on the stage after due preparation. In both forms, dramatisation provides a powerful tool for training the pupils' power of expressive and clear speech and action. Dramatization is also a valuable means of training the pupils to shed off the cloak of stage shyness and face a public audience without nervousness and other inhibitions. It also provides a healthy release for the emotional feelings of the children. Thus, it provides lots of opportunities in which the children's instinctive tendencies to action find a desirable and enjoyable outlet.

(2) **Co-curricular Activities—The Written Aspect, Wall-Paper, Manuscripts and Magazines:** Language has a two-fold function to perform in an individual's daily life.

Communicate through Speech and through Writing: When we talk of teaching English, we have to take into account both the spoken and the written form. The aim of every school is to inculcate in the children the powers of good expression, both oral and written.

Various exercises and experiences in the school curriculum contribute towards improving the expression of children. But even the most conscientious teacher of English will admit that normal school activities are rather inadequate in encouraging the children to express a their views in writing. Even the maximum number of essays and composition exercises done in class are inefficient in providing the child a free rein to express his ideas and opinions on a subject of his choice.

The school wallpaper provides an excellent opportunity for the display of such articles written by the children in sincere and original manner. In such efforts, the child is not constrained by the limitations of classroom discussions or of subjects by the teachers. He can write on anything that catches his fancy or he may express an opinion on any subject that is dear to his heart. The fact that good efforts by the students will have the honour of being displayed on the school wallpaper encourages the child to put in all his best efforts to produce a flawless piece of writing. The wallpaper also encourages the poetic talents of some student which would otherwise have died a natural death in the absence of any favourable wind to nurture the flame of talent. Thus, a wallpaper provides tremendous opportunities and encouragement to children to express their ideas originally and in a presentable manner. A good teacher of English should exploit this part of the school's activity to encourage the children to write as often as they feel the inclination.

The school magazine has all the advantages of the wallpaper and even more. Since all children are greatly interested in what their friends write, the magazine will have a tremendous popular appeal to the children. The teacher of English can exploit this by including some articles on famous books or pieces of literature or poems in such a manner that the children's curiosity is aroused and they are encouraged to go to the source. In this manner, children can be led to great works of literature. The latest book is available in the library and other such useful information can be transmitted through the school magazine. Moreover, the school magazine has the added advantage of having wider circulation. Hence, the standard of articles and poems published can be maintained at a much higher standard. This automatically will raise the standard of writing of the pupils also. Thus, a wall-produced school-magazine fosters good habits of both extra reading and writing in the students.

❒

15

Teaching of Drama

Drama as a subject in its own right does not feature in the National Curriculum and the demands on time that teaching the statutory subjects takes mean that drama, together with other non-statutory subjects, is squeezed into a small time slot. When this first became known there was concern in the ranks of drama teachers, for art and music received honourable mentions and their places in the grand scheme of educational reform was assured.

In the Cox report on English, for ages 5 to 16 (DES/WO, 1989), drama was given an important place within English teaching (although not exclusively within English): 'We would stress, however, that the inclusion of drama methods in English should not in any way replace drama as a subject for specialist study'. However, realistically its future in most schools appears to be as a part of English rather than a subject in its own right. The fact that the report supported drama as a separate subject was lost when the National Curriculum documents were drawn up. Following an invited submission by a small group of drama specialists, the NCC set up a drama Task Group. Their brief was to cover four areas: to look at existing references to drama within the National Curriculum; to provide guidance to teachers and head teachers on the contribution that Drama makes to the curriculum; to consider and advise Council on the elements of drama beyond level 6 which the English Working Group did not define; to provide examples of how schemes of work derived from programmes of study can include drama across shared attainment targets.

This seemed to be quite a promising development, and although the brief was quite restrictive the final document that was produced was more wide ranging and quite substantial. The NCC assured the team that it would be published as 'Curriculum Guidance Number 9' in February 1991. However, this was delayed and it was decided by the NCC that it would publish a circular, which would very briefly outline areas of attainment, in the Spring of 1991 and follow this with the guidance document.

In fact what has been published so far is a Poster (DES, 1991): a poster entitled *'Drama in the National Curriculum',* identifying references to drama in the orders for English, science, technology and history and in the proposals for modern foreign languages. As all these references can be read in the relevant documents anyway, this is certainly not an adequate substitute for the guidance document written by the drama specialists. So what exactly do we have of drama in the National Curriculum? As one would expect, as it has no place of its own, drama is seen as a tool and service subject. The references to 'role-play' found in technology, history, and modern foreign languages are intended to facilitate knowledge development for those particular subjects. They have nothing to do with learning the processes or forms of drama that might be the purpose if the role-plays were part of a drama lesson.

O'Neill's (1983) 'essentialist' quality of Drama as a 'way of knowing' could be employed particularly in a subject like history. But this is something the teacher will have to create independently if the stated intention of a role-play is set out in terms of whether by the end of it a pupil can ask for a kilo of onions, or knows how medieval people bartered grain for land.

As one would expect, the most extensive references to drama come within the English order. However, they relate, in the most part, to a very narrow interpretation of drama and one which many drama specialists would argue is not drama at all. The references can be grouped under the headings: Performance; Text Study/Knowledge; Role-play; Improvisation. As they stand they seem to be reasonable expressions of drama. However, when we look closely at the intended learning outcomes we find that once again drama is being relegated to a position as a tool for achieving particular learning and not as a subject in its own right.

Here is a closer look at some specific references.

Text Study/Knowledge

At Key Stage 1 pupils should 'write in response to a full range of well chosen. . . plays'.

At Key Stage 2 pupils 'should listen and respond to an increasing range of plays' and 'write in response to a wide range of stimuli, including.... plays'.

At Key Stage 3 'Literary texts (including drama scripts).... might furnish many of the materials and topics for discussion for which planned outcomes, *e.g.* in written work or presentations, might emerge'.

At Key Stage 4 pupils should 'write in a wider range of forms, including.... reviews of.... plays,.... playscripts' and recognize and describe some of the 'lexical, grammatical and organisational characteristics of different types of written text, *e.g*.... playscripts'.

The Statements of Attainment list a number of activities that arise from text, such as writing about characters and development of plot, reading a range of fiction and non-fiction including drama, listening and responding to stories and poems.

Although some of these activities purport to be drama, many of them are standard English Literature exercises masquerading as drama. For example dramatic text has always featured on English Literature syllabuses and been read, analyzed and treated exactly like any other form of text. Few English teachers have really got to grips with dramatic text as 'notation' for performance, which is the way in which it would be treated in a drama classroom. The references here continue to treat playscripts in the same way that is texts for study and for learning based firmly in the Literature mode. Although 'presentation' is mentioned once, there is no mention of the facets of text that would be of vital importance to the drama teacher; staging, design, how to make a text work on stage, bringing the text to life. There is considerable room under this heading to make all this work related to the text and more drama orientated and therefore a much stronger and more relevant learning experience: even the most ardent and traditional literature teacher must agree that at some stage the study of dramatic text has to take performance into account.

Performance

At Key Stage 1 pupils should be guided to 'develop the capacity to convey, when reading aloud, the meaning of the text clearly to the listener through intonation and phrasing'.

At Key Stage 2 pupils should 'recite and read aloud in a variety of contexts, with increasing fluency and awareness of audience'.

At Key Stage 3 pupils should be encouraged to work in a 'wider range of situations in which their individual contributions are given greater emphasis, *e.g.*,...planning and taking part in a group presentation, which....might include performance of a playscript for a school production'.

What becomes apparent here is the emphasis on 'performance' which many drama teachers would avoid in drama altogether. While teachers debate the philosophies of drama in Education and the place of performance in it, for drama in English they are being asked to return to something that has more than a hint of traditional 'speech and drama' about it.

Role-play

At Key Stage 1 activities should ensure that pupils 'read in the context of role-play and dramatic play e.g. in the home corner, class shop,...' pupils should be able to participate 'as speakers and listeners in group activities, including imaginative play, *e.g.* play the role of shop-keeper.... in the class shop'.

At Key Stage 2 pupils should have the opportunity to learn how to 'use, and understand the use of, role-play in teaching and learning, *e.g.* to explore an aspect of history'.

All these opportunities for role-play are a means to an end: to teach language skills, to further reading ability, as a means of packaging content, *e.g.* in exploring history. None is first and foremost about drama and the learning that drama can provide.

Improvisation

At Key Stage 1 the range of activities should be designed 'to develop pupils' ability to speak and listen, should include imaginative play and improvised drama'.

At Key Stage 2 activities should include 'simulations and group drama' and pupils should 'be helped to make more extended contributions to group or class discussions and to informal or formal presentation, *e.g.* dramatic improvisation'.

In the Statements of Attainment pupils are expected to: 'produce well-structured pieces of writing, some of which handle demanding subject matter... *e.g.*, ...develop a playscript from an improvisation'.

Of all the categories, this looks the most promising as drama in education. But once again the learning aims limit this category. At Key Stage 1 the 'imaginative play and improvised drama has been given the role of promoting speaking and listening and while that is the aim, the other learning experiences that could be available are relegated or lost altogether'. At Key Stage 2 there is mention of 'simulation and group drama' but it comes in the context of the reference to KS2 under 'role-play', that is as a means of exploring history or a piece of literature, so the content becomes the learning aim, rather than the process itself. At Key Stages 3 and 4 references to improvisation are virtually lost, with the exception of one statement of attainment which uses it only as a stimulus for formal writing. All the many other learning experiences that improvisation can offer, most importantly, those which are unique to drama, are not considered at all.

So the National Curriculum is offering very little to the drama teacher who believes that the value of drama in education is the individual and unique learning it can offer children in schools. What it does is pay lip service to an outdated, ill-defined view of what non-specialists think drama is about and offer drama as a service subject for the foundation subjects. It is certainly not a very satisfactory position for the future of drama in education or for its practitioners.

In 1989, HM Inspectorate published a paper in the Curriculum Matters series, entitled 'Drama from 5 to 16' (DES, 1989). It was hoped that the paper would 'contribute to the continuing debate about the nature of drama in our schools' and set out a framework 'to help schools formulate policies and practices for the teaching and learning of drama appropriate to their pupils'. This was a much more positive document for drama than anything that has come since from government departments.

Although it has some shortcomings (for example it is rather pedestrian in its examination of drama and fails to deal adequately with the unique qualities that drama offers learning), it is a useful starting point for debate. It offers some sense of the range of activities that make up classroom drama and formulates a set of aims and objectives in learning through drama, with the objectives being set out like the Statements of Attainment in the National Curriculum.

For example, by the age of seven, the end of Key Stage 1, children should 'understand and take pleasure in the difference between pretence and reality'. At eleven, the end of Key Stage 2, pupils should 'know how to structure dramatic sequences in order to convey meaning'. While at sixteen, the end of Key Stage 4, pupils should be able to 'try out different ideas or unorthodox approaches in experimenting with improvisation and text'. Thus in this document we are for the first time given some clear guidelines about what the content of drama lessons should be, because we have a set of aims and objectives.

Given the state of the present legislation, what are our own experts telling us now? The debates within drama in education continue to follow 'Drama versus Theatre' lines, as they have for the past decade; despite the two schools of thought becoming less rigid and aspects of the two merging more readily, there is a continued friction:

> We had wrongly assumed that there was now a generally held understanding of theatre as a process which calls on many art forms to create meaning, resulting in a recognition of the symbiotic relationship between theatre and drama, drawing as both do, on dramatic form. That theatre in educational contexts was now widely utilised, not simply as the play or production end goal of process-orientated drama, but as an integral feature of such work; and that the choice of the appropriate way of working was fundamentally tied to an assessment of learning needs rather than any allegiance to process, product or any other camp.
>
> However, it would appear that while the shrillness of debate centred on the supposed dichotomy between drama and theatre has abated, fundamental differences of intent still underlie the surface agreement on mutuality we seem to have achieved.

We have quoted this passage in full because not only does it voice succinctly the underlying friction that exists despite surface appearances, but it also expresses most succinctly the relationship between drama and theatre. It also reminds us once again of the importance of learning aims for the teacher, because it is the aims that will determine the methods, structures and ways of working within the drama lesson.

As Clark and Goode are prominent practitioners it is also worth looking at their definition of drama. They seek to redirect teachers towards drama in education, an arts subject that recognises and uses the 'symbiotic relationship between theatre and drama'. This is the definition they use:

> An essential form of behaviour in all cultures which allows for the exploration of issues and problems central to the human condition and offers the individual the opportunity to define and clarify their own culture. It is a creative group activity in which individuals behave in 'as if' situations as either themselves or as other people. This attitude of the

> participants in the drama process demands a response from others at a direct feeling level. Awareness of the make-believe situation allows them to reflect, make sense and give meaning to their experience....So drama occurs when a group agree to pretend and maintain that pretence in action through the imagined use of people, time and space.

This definition certainly points out more clearly the vast gulf that exists between Drama in the National Curriculum and the Drama of Clark and Goode. And it does not require any imagination to guess behind whom the majority of drama teachers would line up if asked to show their allegiance.

Other influential drama educators still show this underlying difference in approach to the subject in their writing. Neelands writes:

> Drama (in the educational context) is not as concerned with the transmission of theatre-skills as it is with the construction of imagined experience. Imagined experience (controlled by the conventions of game and theatre) is seen as being a particularly efficient context for children to try out and experiment with new ideas, concepts, values, roles and language in action (*i.e.* in the situational context in which they would naturally occur). Drama is to do with the child experiencing rather than with the child performing.

In this view of Drama Neelands is clearly rejecting any notion of drama as encompassing Theatre Arts and even in a more recent publication Structuring Drama Work (1990), which acknowledges more readily the 'symbiotic' relationship between theatre and drama, he maintains a view of drama that is removed from theatre arts and theatre skills. The book sets out very clearly ways of working in Drama lessons. He divides the structure into four sections: context-building; narrative; poetic; reflective. Each structure is described, given 'cultural connections', learning opportunities and examples.

In his rationale, Neelands describes the conventions he uses:

> The conventions and the examples emphasise interactive forms of interchange, even fusion, of the roles of spectator and actor, rather than those conventions associated with performance where the roles of spectator and actor tend to be more clearly defined. The conventions selected are mainly concerned with the process of theatre as a means of developing understanding about both human experience and theatre itself. This may, or may not, later become translated and communicated through performance. The conventions have been chosen to emphasise theatre's traditional role as an educative form of entertainment which responds to a basic human need to interpret and express the world through symbolic form. The conventions recognise that theatre is not taught, rather that our own basic use of theatre in play and other forms of imitative behaviour become refined and developed by experiencing increasingly complex relationships of convention and content. The conventions selected, therefore, form a bridge between spontaneous and innate uses of theatre and the more poetic conventions of performance craft. They are consciously associated with other familiar youth culture forms in order to stress the familiarity and pervasiveness of theatre.

Neelands is at pains to point out that although he is using theatre in his methods and approaches, it is theatre in its broadest sense and not theatre skills as such. This is emphasised in his view that 'theatre is not taught....(but) developed by experiencing'. Experiencing remains the central issue in this philosophy of drama in education.

This view is in marked contrast to that of David Hornbrook, who writes:

> I believe there is a real danger that our well-intentioned efforts to respond to the claims of children's sub-culture

> (their knowledge) we effectively deny them the knowledge through which they can effect change (our knowledge). Under such a scheme, we go to 'Hamlet' at the National Theatre while they must be content with role-playing and improvisation, not only because we designate these latter activities as more relevant to their needs, but also because professionally we are not prepared to make qualitative judgements between the two experiences. Who are we (the argument goes) to impose our middle-class cultural values on working-class children, when their needs are so patently different?

Hornbrook goes on to advocate a syllabus that, in our present understanding, most of us would call theatre arts, or at any rate one containing a strong element of theatre arts:

> I shall have in mind not only the traditionally accepted and familiar mainstream practices of drama-in-education, the creative improvisations and directed role-playing, but all those less publicised manifestations of drama in our schools, such as visits to the theatre and the school play, puppetry and mime, design, play study and theatre technology. All these, and many other aspects of dramatic art evident in schools, have been for too long submerged beneath the prolific advertising of certain favoured methodologies. Dramatic art is strictly non-sectarian. Nothing which can contribute to the making of dramas must be excluded from consideration.

Hornbrook boldly takes a stand against the whatever-you-do-don't-mention-the-theatre brigade. Other drama teachers may sympathize with the belief that there is no difference between 'drama' and 'theatre'. Hornbrook states that 'conceptually there is nothing which differentiates the child acting in the classroom from the actor on the stage in the theatre'.

If he represents a future consensus (and Hornbrook writes very convincingly), a great deal of time has been wasted over internal wrangling about philosophies and methodologies for drama in education. While readers are still reeling from that thought, Hornbrook snakes another of the cornerstones of the field:

> ....although it is true that both actor and child are involved in a process, dramatic art, the outcome of that process, is itself inescapably a product. In more complex forms of drama making, such as the performance of a play in the theatre, many participants with a wide range of specialist skills are likely to have contributed to what we commonly know as the production process. But classroom improvisations also involve a production process, even though, of course, there may never be a formal, enacted presentation. Children experiment with a theme, they rehearse, reject some aspects, try again, abandon the idea. The teacher takes on a role and directs the action, the drama moves forward. Like the artist beginning a painting or the writer a novel, the possibility of arrival is implicit in the very act of starting the journey.

Drama teachers may find this rather startling view very reassuring. Having firmly believed that the process was the purpose, they will have felt very guilty when despite all planning and guiding, classes show far too much interest in 'finishing their play'. It is in fact a much more realistic position to take, to acknowledge the product of Drama in this way, as we have yet to meet a class that was not at some time or other excited by that idea of 'arrival'.

So two of our most prominent drama practitioners are not yet reconciled in their view of what drama-in-education should be about. This tends to leave classroom teachers doing exactly what they have always done, that is, trying to do what they feel to be right with a particular class at a particular time, employing the methodologies and ideas of others when they seem to be useful.

The problem that arises through this complete individualism of teaching is that there is not necessarily any sense of progress or even connection when a child moves from one drama teacher to the next or from one school to the next.

A further recent development is the establishment of 'National Drama'. It was established in 1990 after several years of discussion between the major Drama Associations in order to be 'One Voice for Drama'. Then, instead of having a number of smaller organizations representing different areas of specialism, there would be one, much larger, and therefore stronger association embracing all those involved in drama education. It would include drama teachers, advisers, inspectors, lecturers, theatre-in-education performers and all others with an interest in the field.

The association was mooted on 11 November 1989, which as Armistice Day seems appropriate and symbolic for an attempt to achieve a united voice to speak for the cause of drama. An inaugural conference took place at the end of March 1990, followed by a first major conference in the autumn of 1990, and the election of a committee. It was the intention of the association from the outset to provide not only courses, publications and a forum for discussion for drama practitioners, but also a political voice for drama-in-education. John Boylan, on behalf of the Interim Committee for National Drama wrote in London Drama that 'With Art and Music named as foundation subjects in the National Curriculum, Drama needs a special voice—not several, as in the past—but one' (Boylan, 1990: 9).

In July 1990, London Drama, the journal of the London Drama Association, under the same Editorial Board, became *The Drama Magazine*, the journal of National Drama, and through the early 1990s drama teachers have been uniting to defend their traditions. If drama is to survive and the cut-backs in training be countered, substantial in-service provision will be necessary, as well as research in aspects of drama, funding and support for international contact, and increased liaison with other beleaguered Arts groupings. Such work will require the strong and committed support of all those who believe in drama in education, whether as a process or as performance.

❐

Other Books on

TEXT BOOKS